CHINA

OPPOSING VIEWPOINTS ®

Other Books of Related Interest

CHINA

O P P O S I N G   V I E W P O I N T S ®

James D. Torr, *Book Editor*

Bonnie Szumski, *Editorial Director*
Scott Barbour, *Managing Editor*

OPPOSING
VIEWPOINTS®
SERIES

Greenhaven Press, Inc., San Diego, California

Chinese Characters on Cover Courtesy of: Maxine Huang Feuchter

Library of Congress Cataloging-in-Publication Data

China : opposing viewpoints / James D. Torr, book editor.
    p.   cm. — (Opposing viewpoints series)
    Includes bibliographical references and index.
    ISBN 0-7377-0649-X (pbk.) —
    ISBN 0-7377-0650-3 (lib. bdg.)
    1. China—Social conditions,—1976– 2. China—Economic
conditions,—1976– 3. China—Relations—United States.
4. United States—Relations—China. I. Torr, James D.,
1974– . II. Series.

HN733.5 .C433 2001
306'.0951—dc21   00-064044
                                             CIP

Greenhaven Press, Inc., P.O. Box 289009
San Diego, CA 92198-9009

"Congress shall make
no law...abridging the
freedom of speech, or of
the press."

First Amendment to the U.S. Constitution

The basic foundation of our democracy is the First
Amendment guarantee of freedom of expression. The
Opposing Viewpoints Series is dedicated to the
concept of this basic freedom and the idea that it is
more important to practice it than to enshrine it.

Contents

Why Consider Opposing Viewpoints?

"The only way in which a human being can make some approach to knowing the whole of a subject is by hearing what can be said about it by persons of every variety of opinion and studying all modes in which it can be looked at by every character of mind. No wise man ever acquired his wisdom in any mode but this."

John Stuart Mill

In our media-intensive culture it is not difficult to find differing opinions. Thousands of newspapers and magazines and dozens of radio and television talk shows resound with differing points of view. The difficulty lies in deciding which opinion to agree with and which "experts" seem the most credible. The more inundated we become with differing opinions and claims, the more essential it is to hone critical reading and thinking skills to evaluate these ideas. Opposing Viewpoints books address this problem directly by presenting stimulating debates that can be used to enhance and teach these skills. The varied opinions contained in each book examine many different aspects of a single issue. While examining these conveniently edited opposing views, readers can develop critical thinking skills such as the ability to compare and contrast authors' credibility, facts, argumentation styles, use of persuasive techniques, and other stylistic tools. In short, the Opposing Viewpoints Series is an ideal way to attain the higher-level thinking and reading skills so essential in a culture of diverse and contradictory opinions.

In addition to providing a tool for critical thinking, Opposing Viewpoints books challenge readers to question their own strongly held opinions and assumptions. Most people form their opinions on the basis of upbringing, peer pressure, and personal, cultural, or professional bias. By reading carefully balanced opposing views, readers must directly confront new ideas as well as the opinions of

9

those with whom they disagree. This is not to simplistically argue that everyone who reads opposing views will—or should—change his or her opinion. Instead, the series enhances readers' understanding of their own views by encouraging confrontation with opposing ideas. Careful examination of others' views can lead to the readers' understanding of the logical inconsistencies in their own opinions, perspective on why they hold an opinion, and the consideration of the possibility that their opinion requires further evaluation.

Evaluating Other Opinions

To ensure that this type of examination occurs, Opposing Viewpoints books present all types of opinions. Prominent spokespeople on different sides of each issue as well as well-known professionals from many disciplines challenge the reader. An additional goal of the series is to provide a forum for other, less known, or even unpopular viewpoints. The opinion of an ordinary person who has had to make the decision to cut off life support from a terminally ill relative, for example, may be just as valuable and provide just as much insight as a medical ethicist's professional opinion. The editors have two additional purposes in including these less known views. One, the editors encourage readers to respect others' opinions—even when not enhanced by professional credibility. It is only by reading or listening to and objectively evaluating others' ideas that one can determine whether they are worthy of consideration. Two, the inclusion of such viewpoints encourages the important critical thinking skill of objectively evaluating an author's credentials and bias. This evaluation will illuminate an author's reasons for taking a particular stance on an issue and will aid in readers' evaluation of the author's ideas.

As series editors of the Opposing Viewpoints Series, it is our hope that these books will give readers a deeper understanding of the issues debated and an appreciation of the complexity of even seemingly simple issues when good and honest people disagree. This awareness is particularly important in a democratic society such as ours in which people enter into public debate to determine the common good.

Those with whom one disagrees should not be regarded as enemies but rather as people whose views deserve careful examination and may shed light on one's own.

Thomas Jefferson once said that "difference of opinion leads to inquiry, and inquiry to truth." Jefferson, a broadly educated man, argued that "if a nation expects to be ignorant and free . . . it expects what never was and never will be." As individuals and as a nation, it is imperative that we consider the opinions of others and examine them with skill and discernment. The Opposing Viewpoints Series is intended to help readers achieve this goal.

Greenhaven Press anthologies primarily consist of previously published material taken from a variety of sources, including periodicals, books, scholarly journals, newspapers, government documents, and position papers from private and public organizations. These original sources are often edited for length and to ensure their accessibility for a young adult audience. The anthology editors also change the original titles of these works in order to clearly present the main thesis of each viewpoint and to explicitly indicate the opinion presented in the viewpoint. These alterations are made in consideration of both the reading and comprehension levels of a young adult audience. Every effort is made to ensure that Greenhaven Press accurately reflects the original intent of the authors included in this anthology.

Introduction

"China is a sleeping giant. When it wakes, it will move the world."

—*Napoléon Bonaparte*

In October 1999, the People's Republic of China (PRC) celebrated its 50th birthday. But for the Chinese, 50 years may not mean that much—for while the PRC was officially established after China's 1949 Communist revolution, China has the oldest continuous surviving civilization in the world. Archaeologists have found evidence of Neolithic man in China as far back as 3400 B.C., although historians often mark the beginning of Chinese civilization at the founding of the Shang dynasty in 1766 B.C.

The pride the Chinese take in their ancient civilization probably accounts for some of the tensions in U.S.-China relations. As former secretary of state Henry Kissinger explains, "China is a great country with a 5,000 year history. We're a great country with a 200 year history. . . . The Chinese believe that they staggered through 4800 of their 5000 years without significant advice from the United States, so it is not self-evident to them that they must follow all our prescriptions."

China's initial relations with the West were characterized largely by humiliation at the hands of more technologically advanced European nations. After little contact between East and West throughout the Middle Ages, British traders in the 18th century began preying on the high numbers of opium addicts that were present in Chinese society at the time. The traders sold opium to Chinese addicts for money, and then used that money to purchase Chinese goods. China attempted to ban the importation of opium in 1839 and 1856, but Great Britain and other European nations forcefully opposed the bans. The result was the Opium Wars, which China lost decisively. "Since that fateful encounter," writes history professor Bruce Cumings, "China's central leaders have swayed this way and that in search of a principle for involvement with the West, a way to grow

12

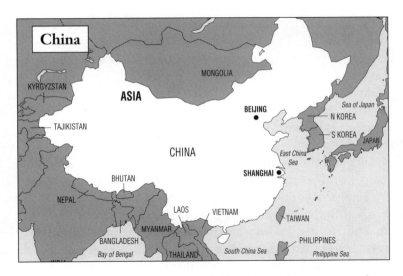

strong while retaining national dignity, to become modern while remaining distinctively Chinese."

In the twentieth century, China underwent two revolutions in its attempts to modernize. The first was in 1912, when peasant uprisings culminated in the end of more than two millennia of imperial rule. A weak republic ruled China until its second revolution in 1949, when Communist leader Mao Zedong declared the People's Republic of China.

Coming at the start of America's cold war with the Soviet Union, China's Communist revolution resulted in a suspension of U.S.-China relations for the next twenty years. Not until 1972, when President Richard Nixon visited China's capital city of Beijing, were relations between the two nations reestablished. Nixon's "opening" of China was only possible because conflicts between China and the Soviet Union led U.S. leaders to view China as something other than a potential enemy.

Even after the fall of the Soviet Union in 1992, the cold war still casts a shadow over U.S.-China relations. The ideological conflicts between communism and capitalism dominate many Americans' views of China. Americans often protest the lack of free elections, free speech, and other human rights in China. They also condemn the PRC government's control over the Chinese economy and call for more free enterprise.

These calls for greater economic freedom, at least, are being answered. China has been instituting substantial free-market reforms since 1978, and as of 2001 boasts one of the fastest-growing economies in the world. This has led to speculation that, sometime in the first quarter of the twenty-first century, China may rival or even surpass the United States as the world's leading economic superpower. David Shambaugh, coauthor of the *The China Reader*, predicts that China and the United States "are likely to be the two dominant world powers during the twenty-first century."

The prospect of China becoming a serious rival to the United States has made it one of the most important areas in U.S. foreign policy. Again, with the legacy of the cold war, some observers believe that conflict between China and the United States is inevitable. The 1997 book *The Coming Conflict with China* describes China as a "long-term adversary." The prospect of China as an enemy is especially worrisome given China's enormous population—approximately 20 percent of all humans on the planet are Chinese. But others are more optimistic: "No doubt China will be a nationalistic superpower that looks after its own interests first," write Daniel Burstein and Arne de Keijzer, authors of *Big Dragon: China's Future*, but they maintain that "China will be a challenge, but it needn't become a threat."

After two centuries of lagging behind the West in terms of industry, economy, and technology, a more modern—and thus more powerful—China is rapidly emerging. The authors in *China: Opposing Viewpoints* examine China's rising power and what it may mean for the United States as well as for the international community in the following chapters: What Are the Most Serious Problems Facing China? What Is the State of Democracy and Human Rights in China? Does China Pose a Threat to the United States? What Principles Should Guide U.S. Foreign Policy Toward China? These chapters debate the myriad factors that U.S. leaders must consider as they face the daunting task of determining U.S. policy on China. As former national security advisor Zbigniew Brzezinski has written, "China is too big to be ignored, too old to be slighted, too weak to be appeased, and too ambitious to be taken for granted."

CHAPTER 1

What Are the Most Serious Problems Facing China?

Chapter Preface

"For most of its 3,500 years of history, China led the world in agriculture, crafts, and science, then fell behind in the 19th century when the Industrial Revolution gave the West clear superiority in military and economic affairs," write the editors of the 1999 *CIA World Factbook*. As the 21st century begins, the country is beginning to modernize its economy, and in the process, is lifting millions of Chinese out of poverty. China is once again taking its place among the world's great powers.

Still, China faces many challenges. For example, the nation's move from an agricultural-based economy to an industrial one is causing enormous environmental problems. In addition, many Chinese are being left behind as China's economy is transformed: From 60 to 100 million surplus rural workers are adrift between the villages and the cities, subsisting on part-time low-paying jobs. Some experts warn that this could lead to political instability in China, as these poor workers begin to demand action from the government.

All these difficulties are exacerbated by the sheer size of China. The nation is home to over 1.2 billion people, roughly one-fifth of the world's total population. Thus, China's most serious problems are occurring on an enormous scale. From air pollution and food shortages to economic or political upheaval, developments in China will inevitably affect the global community. The viewpoints in this chapter examine some of the most pressing problems facing China.

| *"China's coming demographic transformation will bring three sets of serious social problems: rapid aging, declining manpower, and a protracted bride shortage."*

China's Aging Population Will Cause Serious Problems

Nicholas Eberstadt

Nicholas Eberstadt is a visiting fellow of the Harvard Center for Population and Development Studies. In the following viewpoint, he predicts that as China's population ages, the nation will face increasingly serious population-related problems. The first will be that by 2025, the number of elderly in China will be far greater than the number of working adults. The second is that the size of China's work force will shrink, as today's workers age, with proportionately fewer workers to replace them. Finally, because of the practices of sex-selective abortion and female infanticide in China, there are currently more boys than girls in China. By 2025, millions of adult Chinese males will be unable to find a bride and start a family.

As you read, consider the following questions:

1. What was the median age among Chinese in 1997, and what will it be in 2025, according to the author?
2. According to the *Beijing Luntan* essay quoted by Eberstadt, what future social problems will China likely experience as a result of the current disparity between male and female births?

Reprinted from "Demographic Clouds on China's Horizon," by Nicholas Eberstadt, *American Enterprise*, July/August 1998. Reprinted with permission from *American Enterprise*.

W hile there is little about China's position in the year 2025 that we can predict with confidence, one critical aspect of China's future can be described today with some accuracy: her population trends. Most of the Chinese who will be alive in 2025, after all, have already been born.

The most striking demographic condition in China today is the country's sparse birth rate. Though most of the population still subsists at Third World levels of income and education, fertility levels are remarkably low—below the level necessary for long-term population replacement, in fact. This circumstance of course relates to the notorious "One Child" policy of China's Communist government, applied with varying degrees of force for nearly two decades.

Ironically, by laboring so ferociously to avoid one set of "population problems"—namely, "overpopulation"—Beijing has helped to ensure that another, even more daunting set of problems will emerge in the decades ahead. Those population problems will be, for Beijing and for the world, utterly without precedent. While impossible to predict their impact with precision, they will impede economic growth, exacerbate social tensions, and complicate the Chinese government's quest to enhance its national power and security.

Population Growth in China Is Slowing

How can we know fairly well what China's demography will look like 25 years from now? Because according to the latest estimates by the U.S. Bureau of the Census, about a billion of the 1.2 billion Chinese living on the mainland today will still be alive in 2025—accounting for about seven out of every ten of the 1.4 billion Chinese then alive.

The main population wildcard in China's future is fertility. The Census Bureau suggests that the nation's total fertility rate (TFR) now averages a bit under 1.8 births per woman per lifetime (significantly below the 2.1 births necessary for long-term population stability). For broad portions of the Chinese populace, fertility appears to be even lower— as depressed as 1.3 lifetime children per woman in some cities. In Beijing and Shanghai, TFRs may actually have fallen under one by 1995!

The Census Bureau assumes Chinese fertility will average

about 1.8 births per woman through 2025. But today's child-bearing takes place under the shadow of the country's severe—and coercive—antichild campaign. Might not the birth rate leap up if that program were discarded or reversed? It's impossible to be sure, but bits of evidence suggest that a revolution in attitudes about family size has swept China since Mao's death—and that this would prevent fertility from surging back toward more traditional patterns, even if all governmental controls were relaxed. Consequently, the Bureau projects that China will be reaching zero population [growth] 25 years from now.

The "Graying" of China's Population

But China's population will look quite different than it does today, as the nearby chart reveals. China in 2025 will have fewer children: The population under 15 years of age is projected to be almost 25 percent smaller than today. The number of people in their late twenties may drop nearly 30 percent. But persons in their late fifties stand to swell in number by over 150 percent, and there will be more people between the ages of 55 and 59 than in any other five-year age span. Persons 65 years or older are likely to increase at almost 3.5 percent a year between now and 2025, accounting for over three-fifths of the country's population growth.

In short, if Census Bureau projections prove correct, China's age structure is about to shift radically from the "Christmas tree" shape so familiar among contemporary populations to something more like the inverted Christmas trees we see out for collection after the holidays. While in 1997 there were about 80 Chinese age 65 or older for every 100 children under age five, by 2025 China would have more than 250 elderly for every 100 preschoolers.

China's coming demographic transformation will bring three sets of serious social problems: rapid aging, declining manpower, and a protracted bride shortage.

China's "graying" will be as swift as any in history. In 1995, the median age in China was just over 27 years. By 2025 it will be about 40.

Although several European nations are already at China's 2025 median age, they got there much more slowly, and with much more societal wealth available to cushion the effects. A similar "graying" over the last four decades in Japan has emerged as an intense concern of Tokyo policymakers, who wonder how the nation is going to manage its growing burden of pensioners. Like the China of 2025, Japan's median age is currently around 40 years. But Japan is vastly richer today than China could hope to be by 2025. Even if its current brisk pace of economic progress continues, China will still be by far the poorest country ever to cope with the sort of old-age burden it will face.

China's Age Pyramid in 1995 and in 2025

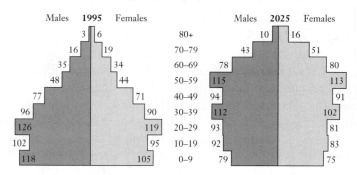

The numbers in the middle column indicate age groups; the numbers along each "tree" indicate the number, in millions, of males and females in that age group.

U.S. Bureau of the Census

For despite its recent progress, China remains a land of daunting economic disparities and crushing poverty. World Bank research has indicated that the proportion of Chinese suffering "absolute poverty" (defined by the Bank as living on less than $1 a day) was nearly 30 percent from 1981–95. Though that figure is undoubtedly lower today, under almost any plausible scenario for future income growth, China in 2025 will still have hundreds of millions of people with incomes not much different from today's average ones—but with a dramatically older population.

How will such a nation care for its elderly? Under current arrangements, the only social security system for most of the country's poor is their family. Scarcely any public or private pension funds operate in the remote rural areas where the overwhelming bulk of China's poor reside. In 2025, grandparents will by and large be the parents of the "One Child" era, so they will have few offspring to offer them shelter in old age. A small but significant group will have no surviving children. A fourth or more could have no surviving sons—thus finding themselves, under Chinese culture, in the unenviable position of depending on the largesse of their son-in-law's household, or, worse, competing for family resources against their son-in-law's parents.

Declining Manpower

Problem two will be declining manpower. Over the past generation, China's brisk economic growth has been partly due to an extraordinary increase in the work force. From 1975 to 1995, China's "working-age population" grew by over 50 percent (or nearly 300 million persons). In a final burst due to population increase, it will grow by over 12 million persons a year at the beginning of the 2000's. Then the growth of potential workers will abruptly brake. By around 2015, China's working-age group will have peaked at just under 1 billion. In 2025, it is projected to be about 10 million persons smaller than a decade earlier. Thereafter, the decline may accelerate, with the workforce shrinking by as many as 70 million people over 15 years.

Having fewer workers may complicate China's quest for economic growth. Younger people tend to be better educated than their elders, and as they stream into a work force this increases its average skill. But China's demographic trends will slow down the improvement in education and skill-levels among the working-age population. Today, the rising cohort of 10- to 14-year-olds represents roughly a seventh of the country's working-age population. By 2015 it will be only a twelfth. This presages a sharp slowdown of education-based improvements in labor productivity.

An Imbalance in the Sex Ratio

China will not be the first country in the world to wrestle with an aging populace or a shrinking workforce. But China's third major demographic challenge is unprecedented: a coming imbalance between men and women of marriageable age.

Beginning with the advent of the nation's "One Child" policy, Chinese sex ratios began a steady, and eerie, rise. By 1995, a Chinese sample census counted over 118 boys under the age of five for every 100 little girls. Part of this imbalance is a statistical artifact—the combination of strict government birth quotas and the strong Chinese preference for sons has caused some parents to hide or "undercount" their newborn daughters, so that they might try again for a boy. But the larger portion of the reported imbalance appears to be real—the consequence of sex-selective abortion and, to a lesser extent, female infanticide.

This tragic imbalance between boys and girls will mean a corresponding mismatch of prospective husbands and brides two decades hence. By Chinese tradition, virtually everyone able to marry does. But the arithmetic of these unnatural sex imbalances is unforgiving, implying that approximately one out of every six of the young men in this cohort must find a bride from outside of his age group—or fail to continue his family line.

In China's past, any problem of "excess" males was generally solved by the practice of marrying a younger bride, which worked well when each new generation was larger than the one before. But with today's low fertility, each new generation in China will typically be smaller than the one before. So if young men try to solve their marriage problem by pairing off with a younger woman, they will only intensify the "marriage crisis" facing men a few years their junior. Nor will searching abroad for a Chinese wife be very promising: By 2020, the surplus of China's twentysomething males will likely exceed the entire female population of Taiwan!

In early modern Europe, bachelorhood was an acceptable social role, and the incidence of never-married men was fairly high. In China, however, there is no such tradition. Unless it's swept by a truly radical change in cultural attitudes toward marriage over the next two decades, China is poised to experience an increasingly intense, perhaps desperate, competition among young men for the nation's limited supply of brides.

Extraordinary Social Strains

A 1997 essay in the journal *Beijing Luntan* predicted direly that "such sexual crimes as forced marriages, girls stolen for wives, bigamy, visiting prostitutes, rape, adultery . . . homosexuality . . . and weird sexual habits appear to be unavoidable." Though that sounds overly dramatic, the coming bride shortage is likely to create extraordinary social strains. A significant fraction of China's young men will have to be resocialized to accept the idea of never marrying and forming their own family. That happens to be a condition in which men often exhibit elevated rates of crime and violence.

Many of China's young men may then be struck by a bitter irony: At a time when (in all likelihood) their country's wealth and power is greater than ever before, their own chances of establishing a family and comfortable future will look poor and worsening. Such a paradox could invite widespread disenchantment.

There is little any future Chinese government will be able to do to address this problem. China's involuntary bachelors will simply have to "handle punishment they have received as a result of . . . the mistakes of the previous generation," suggests the *Beijing Luntan*. How they will accept this remains to be seen—and it will bear directly on the character and behavior of the China that awaits us.

"China may soon emerge as an importer of massive quantities of grain—quantities so large that they could trigger unprecedented rises in world food prices."

China's Growing Population Will Lead to Worldwide Food Shortages

Lester R. Brown

Lester R. Brown is president of the Worldwatch Institute, a nonprofit institute that raises awareness about global environmental problems. In the following viewpoint, excerpted from his book *Who Will Feed China?: Wake-Up Call for a Small Planet,* Brown contends that as China's population grows, valuable cropland will be lost to industrialization. The country will have to import increasing amounts of grain to feed its people, which will lead in turn to worldwide increases in the price of food. China's food shortages will become the world's food shortages, Brown argues, thus sending a "wake-up call" to the rest of the world about the serious global problem of overpopulation.

As you read, consider the following questions:

1. In Brown's view, how will industrialization in China result in less land that is available for raising food crops?
2. In the author's opinion, what is the immediate challenge facing China?

We often hear that the entire world cannot reasonably aspire to the U.S. standard of living or that we cannot keep adding 90 million people a year indefinitely. Most people accept these propositions. Intuitively, they realize that there are constraints, that expanding human demand will eventually collide with the earth's natural limits.

Yet, little is said about what will actually limit the growth in human demands. Increasingly, it looks as though our ability to expand food production fast enough will be one of the earlier constraints to emerge. This is most immediately evident with oceanic fisheries, nearly all of which are being pushed to the limit and beyond by human demand. Water scarcity is now holding back growth in food production on every continent. Agronomic limits on the capacity of available crop varieties to use additional fertilizer effectively are also slowing growth in food production.

A Worldwide Increase in Food Prices

Against this backdrop, China may soon emerge as an importer of massive quantities of grain—quantities so large that they could trigger unprecedented rises in world food prices. If it does, everyone will feel the effect, whether at supermarket checkout counters or in village markets. Price rises, already under way for seafood, will spread to rice, where production is constrained by the scarcity of water as well as land, and then to wheat and other food staples. For the first time in history, the environmental collision between expanding human demand for food and some of the earth's natural limits will have an economic effect that will be felt around the world.

It will be tempting to blame China for the likely rise in food prices, because its demand for food is exceeding the carrying capacity of its land and water resources, putting excessive demand on exportable supplies from countries that are living within their carrying capacities. But China is only one of scores of countries in this situation. It just happens to be the largest and, by an accident of history, the one that tips the world balance from surplus to scarcity.

Analysts of the world food supply/demand balance have recognized that the demand for food in China would climb dramatically as industrialization accelerated and incomes rose. They have also assumed that rapid growth in food production in China would continue indefinitely. But on this latter front, a closer look at what happens when a country is already densely populated before it industrializes leads to a very different conclusion. In this situation, rapid industrialization inevitably leads to a heavy loss of cropland, which can override any rises in land productivity and lead to an absolute decline in food production.

Lessons from Japan, South Korea, and Taiwan

Historically, there appear to be only three other countries that were densely populated in agronomic terms before industrializing—Japan, South Korea, and Taiwan. The common experience of these three gives a sense of what to expect as industrialization proceeds in China. For instance, the conversion of grainland to other uses, combined with a decline in multiple cropping in these countries over the last few decades, has cost Japan 52 percent of its grain harvested area, South Korea 46 percent, and Taiwan 42 percent.

As cropland losses accelerated, they soon exceeded rises in land productivity, leading to steady declines in output. In Japan, grain production has fallen 32 percent from its peak in 1960. For both South Korea and Taiwan, output has dropped 24 percent since 1977, the year when, by coincidence, production peaked in both countries. If China's rapid industrialization continues, it can expect a similar decline.

While production was falling, rising affluence was driving up the overall demand for grain. As a result, by 1994, the three countries were collectively importing 71 percent of their grain.

Exactly the same forces are at work in China as its transformation from an agricultural to an industrial society progresses at a breakneck pace. Its 1990 area of grainland per person of 0.08 hectares is the same as that of Japan in 1950, making China one of the world's most densely populated countries in agronomic terms. If China is to avoid the decline in production that occurred in Japan, it must either be more effective in protecting its cropland (which will not be easy, given Japan's outstanding record) or it must raise grain yield per hectare faster during the next few decades than Japan has in the last few—an equally daunting task, considering the Japanese performance and the fact that China's current yields are already quite high by international standards.

Loss of Cropland and Irrigation Water

Building the thousands of factories, warehouses, and access roads that are an integral part of the industrialization process means sacrificing cropland. The modernization of transportation also takes land. Cars and trucks—with sales of 1.3 million in 1992 expected to approach 3 million a year by the decade's end—will claim a vast area of cropland for roads and parking lots. The combination of continually expanding population and a shrinking cropland base will further reduce the already small area of cropland per person.

At issue is how much cropland will be lost and how fast. Rapid industrialization is already taking a toll, as grain area has dropped from 90.8 million hectares in 1990 to an estimated 85.7 million in 1994. This annual drop of 1.26 million hectares, or 1.4 percent—remarkably similar to the loss rates of China's three smaller neighbors in their industrialization heyday—is likely to endure as long as rapid economic growth continues.

China faces another threat to its food production that its three smaller neighbors did not. Along with the continuing disappearance of farmland, it is also confronted by an extensive diversion of irrigation water to nonfarm uses—an acute concern in a country where half the cropland is irrigated and nearly four-fifths of the grain harvest comes from irrigated land. With large areas of north China now experiencing water deficits, existing demand is being met partly by depleting aquifers. Satisfying much of the growing urban and industrial demand for water in the arid northern half of the country will depend on diversions from irrigation.

An Exceptional Agricultural Record

That China's grain production might fall in absolute terms comes as a surprise to many. This is not the result of agricultural failure but of industrial success. Indeed, China's record in agriculture is an exceptional one. Between 1950 and 1994, grain production increased nearly fourfold—a phenomenal achievement. After the agricultural reforms in 1978, output climbed in six years from scarcely 200 million tons to 300 million tons. With this surge, China moved ahead of the United States to become the world's leading grain producer.

Another way of evaluating China's agricultural record is to compare it with that of India, the world's second most populous country. Per capita grain production in China, which was already somewhat higher than in India, climbed sharply after agricultural reforms were launched in 1978, opening an impressive margin over its Asian neighbor.

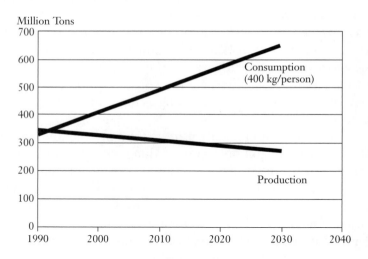

Projected Grain Production and Consumption in China

Lester R. Brown, *Who Will Feed China?*, 1995.

Between 1978 and 1984, China did what many analysts thought was impossible: In just six years, it raised annual grain production from roughly 200 kilograms per person to nearly 300 kilograms. At 200 kilograms, almost all grain is needed to maintain a minimal level of physical activity; an additional 100 kilograms a year opens the way for converting some grain into pork, poultry, and eggs. The immediate challenge facing China is not averting starvation, for it has established a wide margin between its current consumption level of 300 kilograms and the subsistence level. Rather, the challenge is to maintain price stability in the face of soaring demand for food driven by unprecedented advances in income.

Both Population and Prosperity Are on the Rise

While China's food production capacity is starting to erode as a result of its breathtaking pace of industrialization, its demand for food is surging. The country is projected to add 490 million people between 1990 and 2030, swelling its population to 1.6 billion—the equivalent of adding four Japans. Because China's population is so large, even a slow rate of growth means huge absolute increases. Yet these increases are only the beginning of the story.

Even as population expands, incomes are rising at an unprecedented rate. Economic growth of 13 percent in 1992 and again in 1993, of 11 percent in 1994, and of an estimated 10 percent in 1995 adds up to a phenomenal 56-percent expansion of the Chinese economy in just four years. Never before have incomes for so many people risen so quickly.

This rapid economic expansion promises to push demand for food up at a record rate. When Western Europe, North America, and Japan began establishing modern consumer economies after World War II, they were home to some 340 million, 190 million, and 100 million people, respectively. By contrast, China is entering the same stage with a population of 1.2 billion and an economy that is expanding twice as fast. If its rapid economic growth continues, China could within the next decade overtake the United States as the world's largest economy.

Predicting China's Food Demand

Past experience has not prepared us well for assessing the scale of China's future food demand. Multiplying 1.2 billion times anything is a lot. Two more beers per person in China would take the entire Norwegian grain harvest. And if the Chinese were to consume seafood at the same rate as the Japanese do, China would need the annual world fish catch.

As incomes rise, one of the first things that low-income

people do is diversify their diets, shifting from a monotonous fare in which a starchy staple, such as rice, supplies 70 percent or more of calories to one that includes meat, milk, and eggs. As consumption of pork, beef, poultry, eggs, milk, and other livestock products increases along with income, grain requirements rise rapidly.

In neighboring Japan, the soaring demand for grain driven by prosperity combined with the heavy loss of cropland since mid-century to push dependence on grain imports to 72 percent of total grain consumption in 1994. These same forces are now at work in China. It is one thing for a nation of 120 million people to turn to the world market for most of its grain. But if a nation of 1.2 billion moves in this direction, it will quickly overwhelm the export capacity of the United States and other countries, driving food prices upward everywhere.

Warning Signs

The first signs of a growing imbalance between the demand and supply for grain in China became evident in early 1994. In February, grain prices in China's 35 major cities had jumped 41 percent over the same month in 1993. In March, driven by panic buying and hoarding, the rise continued unabated. In response, the government released 2.5 million tons of grain from stocks to check the runaway increase in prices. This calmed food markets, but only temporarily. By October, grain prices were 60 percent higher than a year earlier. More grain reserves were released, and the government banned trading in rice futures on the Shanghai Commodity Exchange. Speculators were driving futures prices upward, leading to panic among urban consumers. The 1994 inflation rate of 24 percent—the worst since modern China was created in 1949—was largely the result of rising food prices.

Resisting the import of grain throughout most of 1994, Beijing let prices rise as much as possible to encourage farmers to stay on the land. In recent years an estimated 120 million people, mostly from the interior provinces, have left the land and moved to cities in search of high-paying jobs. This rootless, floating population, roughly the size of Japan's, wants to be part of the economic revolution. As a potential source of political instability, these migrants are a matter of deep concern in Beijing. The government is trying to maintain a delicate balance, letting the price of grain rise enough to keep farmers on the land but not so much that it creates urban unrest that could lead to political upheaval.

Leaders in Beijing are also trying to deal with massive unemployment and underemployment, with much of the latter masked by villagers eking out a meager existence on tiny plots of marginal land. Creating enough jobs to employ productively an estimated 800 million workers depends on maintaining double-digit or near double-digit rates of economic growth. The government opened the country up to foreign investment in part because it was the only way to get the capital and technology needed to achieve this vital goal.

If China holds together as a country and if its rapid modernization continues, it will almost certainly follow the pattern of Japan, South Korea, and Taiwan, importing more and more grain. Its import needs may soon far exceed the exportable supply of grain at recent prices, converting the world grain economy from a buyer's market to a seller's market. Instead of exporters competing for markets that never seem large enough, which has been the case for most of the last half-century, importers will be fighting for supplies of grain that never seem adequate.

A Wake-Up Call

In an integrated world economy, China's rising food prices will become the world's rising food prices. China's land scarcity will become everyone's land scarcity. And water scarcity in China will affect the entire world.

In short, China's emergence as a massive grain importer will be the wake-up call that will signal trouble in the relationship between ourselves, numbering 5.7 billion [as of 1995], and the natural systems and resources on which we depend. It may well force a redefinition of security, a recognition that food scarcity and the associated economic instability are far greater threats to security than military aggression is.

"The people of China face the challenge of balancing the pace of economic development with the need to protect the environment from further degradation."

China Faces Serious Environmental Problems

Chenggang (Charles) Wang

In the following viewpoint, Chenggang (Charles) Wang describes the environmental problems facing China, which include air pollution and acid rain, water pollution and water shortages, excess garbage, and deforestation. China's problems are so enormous because of the sheer number of people involved, he explains, and will become more severe as the nation industrializes its economy. Wang is a senior scientist at Environmental Elements Corporation and a frequent lecturer on doing business with China.

As you read, consider the following questions:
1. How many of the world's ten most polluted cities are in China, according to the study by the World Health Organization that the author cites?
2. What percent of the river sections near urban areas in China are seriously polluted, according to Wang?
3. What percent of the world's carbon dioxide emissions does Wang say China accounts for?

China is home to more than 1.2 billion people, one-fifth of the global population. In terms of landmass, it stands as the fourth-largest country—after Russia, Canada, and the United States. [In October 1999], as the People's Republic of China celebrates its fiftieth anniversary, it can be proud of its rapid economic growth. At the same time, however, the nation grapples with serious environmental deterioration and depletion of natural resources.

The environmental degradation has become manifest in a surprising number of ways: There is severe pollution of urban air, acid rain deposition in many areas, serious water pollution, a shortage of drinking water, and solid waste pollution. In addition, soil erosion and deforestation are accelerating. Factors that have contributed to this state of affairs include rapid industrialization, inadequate public awareness of environmental protection, and insufficient management by the government. These problems endanger public health and quality of life, and they restrict the nation's economic and social development.

It is important to note that China's recent history is defined by developments pre- and post-1978. From 1949 through the mid-1970s, China was almost totally isolated from the rest of the world, operating under a Soviet-style economy planned by the central government. The Chinese Communist Party and government attempted to move the old China from an impoverished, backward state into a relatively prosperous socialist nation. While this period was marked by a limited degree of success, it included some costly political and economic mistakes, such as the Great Leap Forward of the 1950s and the Cultural Revolution of the '60s. These mistakes seriously damaged China's economy and the environment.

Fortunately, late in 1978, China began pursuing policies of economic reform and openness to the outside world, leading to rapid economic growth. From 1979 to 1996, the gross domestic product (GDP) increased at an average rate of around 10 percent per year. Although the Asian economic crisis of 1997 had a negative effect, China's GDP grew by 8.8 percent in 1997 and 7.8 percent in 1998.

The problem of air pollution in China is twofold: deteriorating quality of urban air and worsening levels of contaminants that cause acid rain. In large cities, people increasingly complain and worry about the quality of air they breathe. A recent study by the World Health Organization reports that 7 of the world's 10 most polluted cities are in China. Beijing is the most contaminated capital in the world and one of the worst cities in China in terms of air quality, according to a recent environmental-inspection report issued by the Environmental and Resources Committee of the National People's Congress.

In urban areas, severe air pollution is caused by the burning of coal, which fuels 75 percent of the nation's energy production, and by emissions from vehicular exhaust and nearby industrial facilities. The major pollutants are particulates and sulfur dioxide. Coal burning accounts for 70 percent of the smoke and dust in the air and 90 percent of sulfur dioxide emissions. And vehicular emissions are responsible for increasing concentrations of nitrogen oxides, hydrocarbons, and carbon monoxide in major cities.

Acid rain, which results from emissions of sulfur dioxide and nitrogen oxides, affects 30 percent of China's land area, especially in the southern regions. It causes over $13 billion in damage to human health, farms, and forests each year.

To curb air pollution, China has recently taken aggressive measures, including the formal establishment in January 1998 of two special control zones (located primarily in northern and southern regions) to monitor acid rain and control sulfur dioxide emissions. All new coal-fired power plants are required to install particulate control devices, such as electrostatic precipitators and fabric filters, which can remove more than 99 percent of particulate emissions. There is also a ban on the digging of new mines that contain high-sulfur coal. In addition, coal washing and flue-gas desulfurization are currently being recommended and will be required by 2010, especially in the two special control zones.

Local governments, as well, are becoming proactive. The Beijing municipal government has adopted 46 measures to actively reduce and strictly control emissions from coal burning and vehicular exhaust. Progress has been made. In April 1999, environmental-monitoring data showed that the concentration of sulfur dioxide was lower than in the same period last year, and the rate of increase of nitrogen oxides concentration had slowed. Beijing also started a new campaign to prevent and control particulate pollution. Heavy industrial plants have been moved out of densely populated urban areas.

About 10 major cities—including Beijing, Shanghai, and Guangzhou—have banned the use of leaded fuel, which will be phased out nationwide by the year 2000. In Beijing, vehicles are required to pass an emissions test before getting on the road. And many large cities have begun to switch from gasoline to cleaner fuels, such as liquefied natural gas and liquefied petroleum gas, for taxicabs and urban mass-transportation fleets.

To raise public awareness of air pollution and its impact, nearly 60 cities in China publish reports on air quality at least once a week. Five of these cities report daily. Newspapers, radios, and even sites on the Internet (such as Shanghai Environmental Online) report on the air-quality index and forecast. Recently, visitors from Beijing to Washington, D.C., expressed their strong desire to take home not American-made products but the clean air that Americans enjoy in their capital!

Water Scarcity and Pollution

China possesses two of the world's longest rivers: the Yangtze (Long River) and the Yellow River. The latter name actually reflects the water's yellow color, caused by a high content of mud and sand from erosion. Yet the country's water resources per capita are only 2,400 cubic meters (84,755 cubic feet)—or one-fourth the world's average. In this respect, China ranks 109th among 149 countries. Over half the 668 cities in China are facing water shortages, with 100 of them suffering severe scarcities. These shortages, particularly acute in the northern regions, are a result of uneven natural distribution of water resources.

Besides water scarcity, there is the problem of pollution of rivers, lakes, and underground water. Factors contributing to this pollution include the country's rapid industrialization and accelerating urbanization, combined with inadequate infrastructure investments, backward technologies, and poor environmental management.

Serious water pollution exists in more than 52 percent of the river sections near urban areas. Roughly two-thirds of the river sections monitored in seven major river systems are severely contaminated with organic pollutants, suspended solids, and ammonia, dramatically altering the quality of drinking water and adversely affecting fisheries. Almost all major lakes have heavy eutrophication [water pollution caused by excessive plant nutrients, often from man-made fertilizers], with high concentrations of nitrogen and phosphorus. There is also an increasing incidence of underground water contamination and overexploitation. As a result, the people of China must either boil their water before drinking or buy bottled water.

A recently released report, China's State of the Environment for 1998, states that 39.5 billion tons of wastewater were discharged last year. Of that, nearly one-half came from domestic sewage. While 87.4 percent of industrial wastewater was treated, only 65.3 percent of the treated water met national standards for industrial wastewater discharge. Less than 10 percent of municipal wastewater was treated. The shortage of municipal wastewater-treatment facilities is a serious setback for efforts to reduce water pollution, especially in many urban areas.

In 1995, the Chinese government launched an intensive campaign to prevent and control water pollution, establishing standards for the discharge of pollutants. Called the Three Rivers, Three Lakes Project, this campaign was designed to cover the three most polluted river basins—Huai, Liao, and Hai Rivers—and three severely contaminated lakes: Taihu, Chaohu, and Dianchi.

As of May 1, 1999, the first phase of the project—affecting the Huai River, Taihu Lake, and Dianchi Lake—was completed, and key pollution sources had met the pollutant-discharge standards. But thousands of other enterprises failed to attain the set standards and have been ordered to suspend production or face permanent closure. Work at Chaohu Lake and at the Liao and Hai Rivers is in progress.

According to the State Council's decisions on several environmental-protection issues, all industrial-pollution sources in the nation will have to meet wastewater-discharge standards by the end of the year 2000 or face closure. In addition, cities with populations over 500,000 will be required to build municipal wastewater plants.

Solid Waste

In 1998, the amount of industrial solid waste generated in China was about 800 million tons. Of that, the comprehensive utilization rate (involving recycling and repeated usage) was 47 percent. In addition, 142 million tons of domestic garbage and 9.74 million tons of hazardous waste were produced in China last year. The discharge and storage of solid wastes affect large areas of land and pose a threat to underground water and drinking water resources.

A rather conspicuous environmental problem in China is known as "white" pollution—the random disposal of lunch boxes, plastic packaging materials, and agricultural membranes, most of which are white. White pollution does more than ruin the beauty of the landscape; it threatens transportation safety and utility operations as well.

Rapid urbanization and the rising population density in urban areas have dramatically escalated the need to treat domestic garbage. Limited storage space, obsolete treatment technologies, and inadequate management threaten the quality of urban life, public health, and economic growth. Most city and suburban landfill fields have nearly reached or exceeded their design limits, and few cities have municipal incineration facilities. Government investment, international cooperation, and technology transfer are eagerly sought to help solve these problems.

Damage to Ecosystems

Although China is the world's fourth-largest country, it has only 7 percent of the world's arable land. It has been estimated that since 1949, one-fifth of China's agricultural land has been lost through soil erosion, deforestation, desertification, and economic development. Soil-erosion areas encompass 3.67 million square kilometers (1.42 million square miles), accounting for 38 percent of the total land area, and they continue to increase at an alarming rate of 2,460 square kilometers (950 square miles) per year.

China's forest coverage is only 13.9 percent—about half the world's average. Deforestation has caused excessive damage to ecosystems and contributed to increased soil erosion and desertification. China has 2.62 million square kilometers (1.01 million square miles) of desert area, amounting to 27 percent of its total land and more than twice its arable land. Desertification has caused an annual economic loss of $6.5 billion. The loss of habitable land for wild animals and plants also threatens the country's biodiversity, which is one of the richest in the world.

During the summer of 1998, several parts of China were hit with severe floods. In particular, the Yangtze River basin

Some of the Most Serious Environmental Threats in the World

Despite dramatic improvements in energy efficiency, China is still contending with some of the most serious environmental threats in the world. These include:

- Over half the population (nearly 700 million people) lacks access to clean water, and consumes drinking water contaminated with animal and human waste that exceeds the applicable maximum permissible levels. Overall only 5 percent of household waste and about 17 percent of industrial waste receive any treatment before entering local irrigation ditches, ponds, lakes, and streams.

- All of China's bodies of water are polluted to various degrees. Serious pollution has been documented in the country's seven major watersheds: Huai, Hai, Liao, Songhua, Chang (Yangtze), Zhu (Pearl) and Huang (Yellow).

- China faces severe deforestation problems, which contributed to the devastating floods during the summer of 1998.

- Air pollution in some Chinese cities is among the highest ever recorded, averaging more than ten times the standard proposed by the World Health Organization.

- Air pollution threatens public health and welfare on a large scale. China's six largest cities—Beijing, Shenyang, Chongqing, Shanghai, Xian, and Guangzhou—rank among the most polluted in the world.

- In Beijing, 40 percent of autos surveyed—and 70 percent of taxis—failed to meet the most basic emission standards.

World Resources Institute, "The Environment and China," 1999.

experienced its biggest flood since 1954, resulting in $24 billion in damages. Such disasters can undoubtedly be attributed not only to unusual weather patterns but to human damage of ecosystems as well. Furthermore, severe deforestation, unscientific land conversion, and illegal logging in the upstream section of the Yangtze River have rapidly broadened soil-erosion areas at an average rate of 5,000 square kilometers (1,930 square miles) per year in the river basin. Chinese environmental experts warn that this river could become the second Yellow River unless urgent measures to reverse this trend are taken.

In November 1998, the State Council approved and promulgated the National Ecological Environmental Construction Plan, which launched a nationwide campaign to protect and regenerate forested land. It included an immediate ban on logging in natural forests and illegal land conversion. The council estimates that it will take 50 years to restore areas that have suffered serious ecological harm and to significantly improve the environment in most areas in China.

Environmental Legislation

China's environmental-protection work began officially in 1973, when the State Council convened the first national meeting on this subject. Since then, the government has established comprehensive environmental legislation, including six laws on pollution prevention and nine on natural-resources protection. These laws have led to 29 environmental-protection regulations, over 70 statutes, and more than 900 local regulations. The government has further promulgated 395 environmental standards. More important, for the first time in China's history, destruction of the environment and natural resources is prosecutable as a criminal offense under the newly revised Criminal Law. China has also intensified the enforcement of environmental regulations and frequently conducts in-depth inspections of pollution sources.

Today, nearly all government agencies and large, state-owned enterprises in China have an environmental bureau or department. Key agencies include the State Environmental Protection Administration (SEPA), which was elevated to the ministry level in March 1998; the National People's

Congress Environmental and Resources Committee; and provincial and municipal environmental-protection bureaus.

Recognizing that economic growth has occurred at the expense of the environment, the Chinese government has chosen to implement a strategy for sustainable development, to protect the environment while developing the national economy. In March 1994, the government approved and promulgated Agenda 21: White Paper on China's Population, Environment, and Development in the Twenty-first Century. This paper states China's overall strategy, measures, and programs of action for sustainable development. In March 1996, China's eighth National People's Congress examined and adopted its ninth Five-Year Plan for National Economic and Social Development and the Outline of the Long-Term Target for the Year 2010. Both the plan and the outline include sustainable development as an important strategy for China's economic and social development.

China spent $8.7 billion on environmental protection last year, a 43.7 percent increase over the prior year. Of that, $5.5 billion was invested in the construction of urban infrastructures, corresponding to a 77.7 percent increase over the 1997 figure. The total environmental-protection expenditure as a percentage of the GDP increased from 0.73 percent in 1986–1990, to 0.83 percent during 1990–95, and to nearly 1 percent in 1998—more than in any other developing country, according to the head of China's SEPA. These rising investments reflect the government's commitment to tackling the nation's serious environmental-pollution problems.

Outlook for the Twenty-First Century

A sound environment is an important aspect of the quality of life and a responsibility of the current generation to future generations. Realizing this, the Chinese government has instituted a series of important environmental-protection measures, including the Three Rivers, Three Lakes Project (mentioned earlier) and the Trans-Century Green Projects. These projects appear to be meeting their targets. For instance, by the end of 1998, 438 projects (or 30 percent) of the latter group were completed at a cost of $2.8 billion. Meanwhile, 474 additional projects are under construction, with a planned investment of $13 billion.

In addition to domestic challenges, China faces worldwide issues such as global climate change. The country has signed and joined 18 international environmental conventions, including the [United Nations] Framework Convention on Climate Change. Primarily due to its high dependence on coal, China accounts for 13 percent of the world's carbon dioxide emissions today. At this level, it is the world's second-largest emitter of carbon-containing compounds, after the United States (which generates 23 percent). As an important member of the international community, China has signed bilateral environmental-cooperation agreements with 23 other countries to improve and protect the global environment.

During the summit between Presidents Clinton and Jiang in October 1997, a comprehensive agreement for cooperation on energy and the environment between the two countries was signed. Then in April 1999, Chinese Premier Zhu and Vice President Gore cochaired the U.S.-China Forum on Environment and Sustainable Development in Washington, D.C. In addition, administrators of the U.S. Environmental Protection Agency and China's SEPA have exchanged visits and discussed initiatives for cooperation on air quality and energy efficiency. Successful U.S.-China bilateral cooperation on energy and the environment can benefit both countries and eventually the whole world.

As we stand at the threshold of the twenty-first century, the people of China face the challenge of balancing the pace of economic development with the need to protect the environment from further deterioration. It is likely that China will continue to experience serious air and water pollution, as well as other environmental problems, during the early part of the [twenty-first] century. But the country can meet both economic and environmental goals by implementing a sustainable development strategy, improving public awareness in the area of environmental protection, vigorously enforcing relevant laws and regulations, applying new technologies, and enhancing international cooperation. By combining these efforts, the people of China can look forward to achieving their dream of blue skies, clean water, and unpolluted soil.

"[Continued economic growth in China is] likely to occur only if China continues to make major reforms to its economy."

China Faces Serious Economic Problems

Wayne M. Morrison

China has become one of the world's fastest growing economies, asserts Wayne M. Morrison in the following viewpoint. Since 1979, China has been moving away from its communist state-controlled economy, adopting some principles of free trade, and privatizing many businesses. The country's move toward free markets must continue, warns Morrison, if China is to overcome the many problems associated with its previously stagnant economy, which include inadequate energy and transportation systems as well as regulations that continue to inhibit free trade. Morrison is a researcher in the economics division of the Congressional Research Service, part of the Library of Congress.

As you read, consider the following questions:

1. What are some of the economic reforms that Morrison says Chinese leaders initially instituted in 1979?
2. What type of business accounts for one-third of Chinese industrial production, according to the author, and what problems are associated with them?
3. How does the author describe China's "iron rice bowl"?

Excerpted from *Congressional Research Service Issue Brief for Congress: China's Economic Conditions*, by Wayne M. Morrison for the National Council for Science, December 1, 1999.

P rior to 1979, China maintained a centrally planned, or command, economy. A large share of the country's economic output was directed and controlled by the state, which set production goals, controlled prices, and allocated resources throughout most of the economy. During the 1950s, all of China's individual household farms were collectivized into large communes. To support rapid industrialization, the central government during the 1960s and 1970s undertook large-scale investments in physical and human capital. As a result, by 1978 nearly three-fourths of industrial production was produced by centrally controlled state-owned enterprises (SOEs) according to centrally planned output targets. Private enterprises and foreign invested firms were nearly non-existent. A central goal of the Chinese government was to make China's economy relatively self-sufficient. Foreign trade was generally limited to obtaining only those goods that could not be made or obtained in China.

China's real GDP [gross domestic product] grew at an estimated average annual rate of about 5.3% from 1960–1978. However, government policies kept the Chinese economy relatively stagnant and inefficient, mainly because there were few profit incentives for firms and farmers, competition was virtually nonexistent, and price and production controls caused widespread distortions in the economy. Chinese living standards were substantially lower than those of many other developing countries. The Chinese government hoped that gradual reform would significantly increase economic growth and raise living standards.

The Introduction of Economic Reforms

Beginning in 1979, China launched several economic reforms. The central government initiated price and ownership incentives for farmers, which enabled them to sell a portion of their crops on the free market. In addition, the government established four special economic zones for the purpose of attracting foreign investment, boosting exports, and importing high technology products into China. Additional reforms followed in stages that sought to decentralize economic policymaking in several economic sectors, especially trade. Economic control of various enterprises was given to provincial and local governments, which were generally allowed to operate and compete on free market principles, rather than under the direction and guidance of state planning. Additional coastal regions and cities were designated as open cities and development zones, which allowed them to experiment with free market reforms and to offer tax and trade incentives to attract foreign investment. In addition, state price controls on a wide range of products were gradually eliminated.

Since the introduction of economic reforms, China's economy has grown substantially faster than during the pre-reform period. Chinese statistics show real GDP from 1979 to 1998 growing at an average annual rate of 9.8%, making China one the world's fastest growing economies. According to the World Bank, China's rapid development has raised nearly 200 million people out of extreme poverty. . . .

Trade Between the U.S. and China

According to Chinese trade data, its top five trading partners in 1998 were Japan, the United States, the European Union (EU), Hong Kong, and South Korea. Chinese data show the United States as China's second largest destination for its exports and the third largest source of its imports. China's trade with many of its Asian trading partners fell in 1998, while trade with the United States and the EU rose. . . .

Based on U.S. data on Chinese exports to the United States . . . , and Chinese data on total Chinese exports, it is estimated that Chinese exports to the United States as a percentage of total Chinese exports grew from 15.3% in 1986 to an estimated 38.7% in 1998. This would indicate that the United States is by far China's largest export market. The importance of the U.S. market for China's exports appears to have increased markedly in 1998, likely due to the effects of the global financial crisis (i.e., U.S. imports from China have continued to rise, but imports by several East Asian economies from China have fallen). . . .

Major Challenges Facing the Chinese Economy

China's economy has shown remarkable economic growth over the past several years, and many economists project that it will enjoy fairly healthy growth in the near future. Standard and Poor's DRI, a private international forecasting firm, projects China's GDP will grow at an average annual rate of about 7 percent between 1999 and the year 2005. Economists caution, however, that these projections are likely to occur only if China continues to make major reforms to its economy. Failure to implement such reforms could endanger future growth.

• *State-owned enterprises (SOEs)*, which account for about one-third of Chinese industrial production and employ nearly two-thirds of urban workers, put an increasingly heavy strain on China's economy. Over half are believed to lose money and must be supported by subsidies, mainly through state banks. Government support of unprofitable SOEs diverts resources away from potentially more efficient and profitable enterprises. In addition, the poor financial state of many SOEs makes it difficult for the government to reduce trade barriers out of fear that doing so would lead to wide-spread bankruptcies of many SOEs.

• *The banking system* faces several major difficulties due to its financial support of SOEs and failure to operate solely on market-based principles. China's banking system is regulated and controlled by the central government, which sets interest rates and attempts to allocate credit to certain Chinese firms. The central government has used the banking system to keep afloat money-losing SOEs by pressuring state banks to provide low-interest loans, without which a large share of the SOEs would likely go bankrupt. Currently, about 70% of state-owned bank loans now go to the SOEs, even though a large share of loans are not likely to be repaid. The high volume of bad loans now held by Chinese banks (estimated to total $250 billion) poses a serious threat to China's banking system. Three out of the four state commercial banks are believed to be insolvent. The precarious financial state of the Chinese banking system has made Chinese reformers reluctant to open its banking sector to foreign competition. Corruption poses another problem for China's banking system because loans are often made on the basis of political connections. In many cases, bank branches extend loans to firms controlled by local officials, even during periods when the central government has attempted to limit credit. Such a system promotes widespread inefficiency in the economy because savings are generally not allocated on the basis of obtaining the highest possible returns. In addition, inability to control the credit policies of local and provincial banks has made it very difficult for the central government to use monetary policy to fight inflation without causing major disruptions to the economy.

• *Infrastructure bottlenecks*, such as inadequate transportation and energy systems, pose serious challenges to China's ability to maintain rapid economic growth. China's investment in infrastructure development has failed to keep pace with its economic growth. The World Bank estimates that transportation bottlenecks reduce China's GDP growth by 1% annually. Chronic power shortages are blamed for holding China's industrial growth to 80% of its potential. Transportation bottlenecks and energy shortages also add inflationary strains to the economy because supply cannot keep up with demand.

• *The lack of the rule of law* in China has led to widespread government corruption, financial speculation, and misallocation of investment funds. In many cases, government "connections," not market forces, are the main determinant of successful firms in China. Many U.S. firms find it difficult to do business in China because rules and regulations are generally not consistent or transparent, contracts are not easily enforced, and intellectual property rights are not protected (due to the lack of an independent judicial system). The lack of rule of law in China limits competition and undermines the efficient allocation of goods and services in the economy. In addition, the Chinese government does not accept the concept of private ownership of land and assets in China.

• *High trade barriers* are maintained by the government in large part to protect domestic firms from foreign competition. Such policies have two main negative effects: First, they give domestic firms less incentive to improve productivity and efficiency. Second, restricting competition raises prices and product choices for Chinese consumers of both domestic and imported goods.

• *A wide variety of social problems* have arisen from China's rapid economic growth and extensive reforms, including pollution, a widening of income disparities between the coastal and inner regions of China, and a growing number of bankruptcies and worker layoffs. This poses several challenges to the government, such as enacting regulations to control pollution, focusing resources on infrastructure development in the hinterland, and developing modern fiscal and tax systems to address various social concerns (such as poverty alleviation, health care, education, worker retraining, pensions, and social security).

Chinese Economic Initiatives Announced in 1998

At a news conference in March 1998, newly appointed Chinese Premier Zhu Rongji outlined a number of major new economic initiatives and goals for reforming China's economy and maintaining healthy economic growth, including:

- In 1998, achieve a GDP growth rate of 8%, keep inflation below 3%, and not devalue China's currency.
- Respond to the effects of the Asian financial crisis by expanding domestic demand, especially through increased spending on infrastructure, and by maintaining the pace of previously planned economic reforms.
- Reform and restructure loss-making medium-and-large-sized state-owned enterprises (SOEs) to make them profitable. Reorganize the banking system to increase the regulatory and supervisory power of the central bank and make commercial banks operate independently. Substantially reduce the size of the government and reorganize the remaining government institutions. All three goals are to be obtained within three years.
- Commercialize government housing, reform the health insurance system, improve the system for circulating grain, rationalize the system for approving investment and finance projects, and improve tax collection. . . .

Zhu Rongji's economic plan has been viewed by many analysts as representing the most significant restructuring of the economy to date, since it would substantially reduce the size of the government and diminish its control over various sectors of the economy, dismantle much of the remaining "iron rice bowl" of cradle-to-grave benefits for government and SOE workers, enable banks to make loans on a commercial, rather than political basis, and force a large share of SOEs to operate according to free-market principals. Implementation of such policies would take China significantly closer towards a functioning market economy.

Reform of State-Owned Enterprises. The Chinese leadership has been talking about undertaking major reforms of unprofitable SOEs for the past several years, but has been hesitant to act due to concerns that reforms would lead to widespread bankruptcies and cause political instability. However, the Chinese government has acknowledged that support of SOEs has put a heavy drain on the economy and cannot be maintained indefinitely. As a result, reform of SOEs has been made a top priority. In September 1997, Chinese President Jiang Zemin stated that China would take steps which, if implemented, would essentially privatize (although referred to by the Chinese as "public ownership") all but 1,000 out of an estimated 308,000 SOEs by cutting off most government aid and forcing them to compete on their own. . . .

China's Socialist Legacy

Most of China's economic problems . . . are homegrown—the result of its disastrous socialist legacy, which impoverished and starved millions. The leadership is well aware of its dilemma, though. As one official remarked: "To not reform is to wait for death—to speed up reform is to look for death." The leaders know that economic reform is essential, but they are also aware that reform will cause mass unemployment and social unrest, which could threaten their rule. . . .

China would be wise to look at the recent history of Indonesia, where a one-party system collapsed (fortunately with little bloodshed) almost overnight due to economic mismanagement and corruption. If the leadership in Beijing is not careful, Indonesia's history will be China's future.

Mark A. Groombridge, *World & I*, October 1999.

It is not clear how the Chinese government intends to deal with the problem of displaced workers (likely to total several millions) when and if the SOE reform plan is fully implemented. Chinese officials may be anticipating that continued rapid economic growth will provide new jobs for most displaced workers and that overseas investors will play a major role in restructuring the SOEs by becoming joint owners. *Reform of the Banking System.* Chinese officials have indicated a desire to strengthen and reform its banking system. On January 16, 1998, the central government announced it would attempt to implement new reforms to enhance the power of the central bank over the provincial and state banks and to improve the management systems of all Chinese banks. Such reforms would attempt to lessen the power of local officials to pressure banks into making "bad loans." In addition, the government has indicated that banks will be allowed to make bank loan decisions based on commercial considerations. Finally, on March 2, 1998, the government announced plans to issue bonds to recapitalize the state banks to enable them to write off bad loans. Chinese officials claim their long-term goal is to develop a modern banking system similar to that of the U.S. Federal Reserve system. However, due to the precarious nature of its banking system, Chinese officials appear hesitant to allow foreign banks to expand their operations in China, due to concerns that doing so would force many Chinese banks into bankruptcy.

Infrastructure Development. The Chinese government anticipates that banking and SOE reforms will lead to widespread layoffs. Stimulating domestic demand, especially through infrastructure development, is viewed as a key mechanism to re-employ workers displaced by reforms. Chinese officials announced in February 1998 their intentions to spend $750 billion on infrastructure development over the next 3 years; in September 1998, Chinese officials indicated that $1.2 trillion would be spent. Many analysts, however, have questioned China's ability to obtain funding for such a massive financial undertaking in such a short period of time. The issuance of government bonds has become a major source of finance for infrastructure. However, such policies will likely increase the size of the central government's budget deficit. It is also likely that China hopes to attract foreign investment for much of its infrastructure needs. . . .

China's Accession to the World Trade Organization

China has made its accession to the World Trade Organization (WTO) a major priority for a number of reasons. First, it would represent international recognition of China's growing economic power. Second, it would enable China to play a major role in the development of new international rules on trade in the WTO. Third, it would give China access to the dispute resolution process in the WTO, reducing the threat of unilateral trade sanctions against China or other unilateral restrictions on Chinese exports (such as textile quotas and antidumping duties). Fourth, it would make it easier for reformers in China to push liberalization policies if they could argue that such steps are necessary to fulfill China's international obligations. Finally, China hopes it would gain it permanent [most favored nation (MFN)/normal trade relations]treatment from the United States.

Several arguments have been made by policymakers of current WTO member countries for allowing China into the WTO. First, China is the largest economic and trade power not a member of the WTO. The World Bank projects that China's share of world trade will account for 10% of the world's trade by the year 2020 and that China will become the world's second largest trading nation after the United States. Hence, it is argued that China's trade is too significant to remain outside multilateral trade rules. Second, WTO membership would require China to reduce a wide variety of trade barriers and, hence, would likely create substantial new trade opportunities in China. Third, once China is in the WTO, it would be required to provide extensive information about its trade regime, which would make it very difficult for China to impose new trade and investment barriers. Fourth, the United States (and other WTO members) would be able to bring trade disputes to WTO dispute resolution instead of having to rely on threats of unilateral trade sanctions. Finally, China's accession might enable Taiwan to eventually join the WTO (as a separate customs territory). China has insisted that Taiwan can get into the WTO only after China does. . . .

The Outlook for China's Economy

Despite the relatively shaky state of the Chinese economy, the Chinese government appears to have shown greater willingness to reform China's economic and trade regimes in order to obtain WTO membership. For China, greater market openness would boost competition, improve productivity, and lower costs for consumers, as well as for firms using imported goods as inputs for production. Economic resources would be more likely redirected away from money-losing activities towards more profitable ventures, especially those in China's growing private sector. As a result, China would likely experience more rapid economic growth (than would occur under current economic policies). Greater openness would also boost foreign investment in China, and increase trade flows (both exports and imports). [The investment firm] Goldman Sachs estimates that WTO membership would double China's trade and foreign investment levels by the year 2005 and raise GDP by an additional 0.5% per year.

In the short run, however, widespread economic reforms (if implemented) could result in disruptions in certain industries, especially unprofitable SOEs, due to increased foreign competition. As a result, many firms would likely go bankrupt and many workers could lose their jobs. How the government handles these disruptions will strongly determine the extent and pace of future reforms. The central government appears to be counting on trade liberalization to boost foreign investment and spur overall economic growth; this would enable laid-off workers to find new jobs in high growth sectors. However, the Chinese government is deeply concerned with maintaining social stability. If trade liberalization was followed by an economic slowdown, leading to widespread bankruptcies and layoffs, the central government might choose to delay (or even rescind) certain economic reforms rather than risk possible political upheaval.

*"For China's leaders chaos and instability
have never been abstractions."*

China Faces the Threat of Political Instability

Robert D. Kaplan

As Robert D. Kaplan explains in the following viewpoint,
China's long history includes periods in which the populace
has revolted against a weak central government, and periods
in which "warlord" regimes have ruled with an iron fist. Kaplan argues that China is currently coming out of a "warlord" phase—the government of Mao Zedong's Communists. As the Chinese government becomes less totalitarian,
Kaplan notes, its control over China's huge population will
weaken. He warns that if economic and social conditions in
China worsen, civil strife could result. Kaplan is a corre-
spondent for the *Atlantic Monthly* and the author of several
books, including *An Empire Wilderness*.

As you read, consider the following questions:
1. According to Jack A. Goldstone, as quoted by Kaplan,
   what combination of forces was behind both the
   Tiananmen Square uprising and past Chinese revolts?
2. In Kaplan's opinion, what were the demonstrators in the
   1989 Tiananmen Square uprising most concerned with?
3. What similarities exist between China today and China
   during the late Ming and late Qing dynasties, in the
   author's view?

Excerpted from "China: A World Power Again," by Robert D. Kaplan, *Atlantic
Monthly*, August 1999. Reprinted with permission from *Atlantic Monthly*.

W here China ends, mountains, deserts, and nomadism begin. China's historical borders extend to the edge of arable land in the eastern half of Asia: the Himalayas to the southwest, the Gobi wastes to the north, and the Central Asian khanates (which is what these new post-Soviet states really are) to the west. Its sheer size has meant that China's dynastic transitions have been vulnerable to rebellions, warlordism, and a weak central government. The Ming and Qing Dynasties both collapsed because population growth led to worsening poverty among peasants and more prosperity among merchants and landowners: the peasants revolted against their poverty, and the wealthier stratum revolted against imperial control and taxation.

The Lessons of Tiananmen Square

The same vulnerability persists today. Jack A. Goldstone, in a paper for the Peace and Conflict Studies Program at the University of Toronto, writes,

> The combination of forces revealed in the Tiananmen Square Uprising of [June 4,] 1989—a coalition of merchants, entrepreneurs, urban workers, students and intellectuals, with some support from within the regime, in revolt against a government that survived only because of continued loyalty of key military and bureaucratic leaders—is quite similar to that of past patterns of Chinese revolt.

The lessons that China's leaders learned from Tiananmen Square were from their own history. They knew that, as in the past, many of the demonstrators were more concerned about economic conditions than about freedom per se. They also knew that anarchy in former times, from the Ming rebellions to Mao Zedong's Great Cultural Revolution, cost millions of lives. Western journalists and intellectuals who have been raised in secure, upper-middle-class environments may call for China to welcome a bit of instability for the sake of change, but for China's leaders chaos and instability have never been abstractions. Deng Xiaoping, China's ruler in 1989, lived with the memory of his son's having been forced to jump from an upper-story window by a crowd during the Cultural Revolution.

To satisfy the population while preventing chaos, after

Tiananmen the Communist Party opened up both the economy and the society—the former much more than the latter. In the past decade probably more people in China have seen their material lives dramatically improve than ever before in recorded history, even as democracy has led to social collapse and mafia rule in Russia. The Chinese have also experienced a dramatic increase in personal freedom. Two China experts, David M. Lampton, of the Johns Hopkins School of Advanced International Studies, and Burton Levin, a former ambassador to Burma, have observed that the Communist Party has gone from controlling every facet of daily life in China to controlling the media and the political opposition. Chinese can travel, buy any books and videos they want, open bank accounts, live together if they are gay or unmarried, and so on.

A Liberalizing Regime

It has been a long time since the Chinese people have experienced such a degree of security and freedom. Early in this century, following the 1911 collapse of the Qing Dynasty, China was roiled by mob violence; the Nationalist leader Chiang Kai-shek was only the first among equals in a nation ruled by warlords. Then came the Japanese devastation of China in the Second World War, with some 10 million Chinese casualties. In 1949 Mao Zedong's Communists came to power, unleashing decades of mass murder and government-inflicted famine. Now the most liberalizing regime in Chinese history is the one most attacked by the U.S. media, politicians, and intellectuals—the same groups that in many cases tolerated both Mao's and Chiang Kai-shek's abuses.

Westerners defend their intolerance of China's regime by claiming that new standards of behavior now obtain worldwide, owing to the West's victory in the Cold War and heightened concern about human rights. Even by those standards China's leaders might be singled out for qualified praise: they effectively dismantled communism in the 1980s, years before the Berlin Wall collapsed. The Tiananmen uprising was to no small degree a reaction to the economic dislocations caused by China's early post-communism. At present the so-called Communist Party in China has less control

The Coming Collapse of
Chinese Communism

China shows every sign of a country approaching crisis: a burgeoning population and mass migration amid faltering agricultural production and worker and peasant discontent—and all this as the state rapidly loses its capacity to rule effectively. . . .

It is doubtful that the collapse of communism in China can be averted; indeed, it is not clear that it should be averted. Rather, as with the demise of the Communist party in the USSR, the problem is how best to anticipate that collapse and prevent it from triggering international crises. Given that China's population problems will force major economic adjustments, that such reforms are likely to intensify confrontations among party factions, elites, workers, and other groups, and that the communist leadership appears unwilling to grant the democratic reforms that might win it renewed support, we can expect a terminal crisis within the next 10 to 15 years.

Observers in the West were startled by the suddenness of the USSR's collapse. There will be no excuse for making the same mistake with China. Even while welcoming the likely demise of communism in China, it is essential to begin planning and seeking international agreement on policy options for dealing with the conflicts that will arise as a result of China's transformation. Otherwise, our pursuit of short-term stability will leave us at the mercy of long-term chaos.

Jack A. Goldstone, *Foreign Policy*, Summer 1995.

of its nation's economy than the governments of France and Italy have of theirs. Russia and some of the prospective members of NATO from the former Warsaw Pact have yet to undergo the kind of entrepreneurial revolution China has already accomplished. Indeed, if the country is not liberalizing fast enough, that's news to Motorola, which assumes that China will be the world's biggest market for cell phones in the early twenty-first century.

Weakening Control

Whereas the media often reduce China to a government that oppresses dissidents, the real story is almost the reverse: in fostering economic success since 1989, China's rulers have unleashed social forces that significantly weaken their control. As in the late Ming and late Qing Dynasties, there has been tremendous population growth. The one-child policy collapsed more than a decade ago, and China's population may now be close to 1.5 billion. Population pressure on arable land has led to scarcity and to farmers' revolts against corrupt officials. As the amount of arable land shrinks, the regime cannot prevent many millions of citizens from migrating to urban areas. Yet, as Goldstone points out, urban growth will only expand the numbers and the leverage of the students and business elites who are likely to demand further democratization. Thus, like previous Chinese dynasties, this one will be increasingly beset by both poor farmers and wealthy merchants. The near-double-digit annual growth in China's gross domestic product has generated a new subproletariat of low-paid factory and construction laborers—a historically volatile class, full of frustrated ambition and yearning. The more than 100 million unemployed workers could still bring chaos on a significant scale. Drug smuggling, gambling, prostitution, pickpocketing, and other criminal activities flourish. The issue is not how much control the Beijing regime has but how little.

Given that China is chronically short of water and has one of the highest air-pollution indexes in the world, and also that two thirds of the population lives in flood zones, Party rulers have little margin for error. For all China's problems the West has the same easy answer it had during the violence of the warlord-dominated 1920s: democracy. But democracy in a country with roughly five times the population of the United States, a tiny middle class, and grave ethnic disputes could shred the relative social peace that the Party has for the most part maintained during a mammoth economic transition.

Periodical Bibliography

The following articles have been selected to supplement the diverse views presented in this chapter. Addresses are provided for periodicals not indexed in the *Readers' Guide to Periodical Literature*, the *Alternative Press Index*, the *Social Sciences Index*, or the *Index to Legal Periodicals and Books*.

Economist	"The Ageing of China," November 21, 1998. Available from 25 St. James's St., London, UK, SW1A 14G.
Elizabeth Economy	"Painting China Green," *Foreign Affairs*, March/April 1999.
Jack A. Goldstone	"The Coming Chinese Collapse," *Foreign Policy*, Summer 1995.
Mark A. Groomsbridge	"China's Mixed Economy," *World & I*, October 1999.
Bob Herbert	"China's Missing Girls," *New York Times*, October 30, 1997.
Mark Hertsgaard	"Our Real China Problem," *Atlantic Monthly*, November 1997.
Charles D. Lane	"Disorderly Conduct: Dictatorship Is the Real Threat to China's Stability," *New Republic*, November 24, 1997.
Floris Jan van Luyn	"A Hunger for More than Rice," *World Press Review*, March 1996.
John Pomfret	"China Losing 'War' on Births," *Washington Post*, May 3, 2000.
Elisabeth Rosenthal	"China, Land of Heavy Smokers, Looks into Abyss of Fatal Illness," *New York Times*, November 20, 1998.
Jonathan D. Spence	"In Search of the New China," *Fortune*, October 11, 1999.
Arthur Waldron	"Handwriting on the Wall," *National Review*, May 31, 1999.
Sheryl WuDunn	"The Greatest Leap," *New York Times Magazine*, May 16, 1999.

CHAPTER 2

What Is the State of Democracy and Human Rights in China?

Chapter Preface

On May 4, 1989, approximately 100,000 students and workers marched through Beijing demanding democratic reforms in the government and the removal of the Chinese Communist Party leader, Deng Xiaoping. On May 20, the government declared martial law, and on June 3 and 4, troops were sent into Tiananmen Square, a historic site in the capital city, to stop the protests. The People's Liberation Army, as the Chinese army is called, crushed the demonstrations, killing hundreds and injuring thousands more. Following the violence, the government arrested, imprisoned, and executed many suspected dissidents.

In the West, the violence at Tiananmen Square was reported as the "Tiananmen Square Massacre." Images of soldiers in tanks pursuing students with protest signs left little doubt in Americans' minds about the lack of democracy in China.

While most American observers have condemned the Chinese government's human rights abuses, some suggest that the government's crackdowns on dissent are necessary. Author Robert D. Kaplan argues, "Were China to have suddenly become a parliamentary democracy in 1989 at the time of the Tiananmen Square uprising, the average Chinese citizen would likely be worse off today." By maintaining political stability, Kaplan argues, Chinese leaders were able to encourage economic growth, which will, in his view, eventually pave the way for democratic reforms in China.

In contrast to Kaplan's rather optimistic view of Tiananmen, notable groups such as Human Rights Watch and Amnesty International continue to document the arrests, tortures, and executions that occur routinely in China. In their view, the international community should condemn China's poor record on human rights and use economic sanctions or other pressures to encourage China to become more democratic.

The authors in the following chapter examine the state of democracy and human rights in China and debate whether the nation has made any progress in these areas since the Tiananmen Square uprising.

*"It is a good thing that China became rich,
. . . for a richer China will become more
democratic."*

China Is Becoming More Democratic

Henry S. Rowen

Henry S. Rowen is a professor of public policy and management at the Graduate School of Business at Stanford University. In the following viewpoint, he maintains that the People's Republic of China is on its way to becoming a democracy. Rowen predicts that China will follow the examples of Taiwan and South Korea, which became more democratic as their economies improved. The government is allowing local elections to be held in villages, he notes, and is also beginning to institute fair laws regarding business transactions and the treatment of criminals. Rowen concludes that China is becoming freer each year, and will continue to do so as long as it becomes more prosperous.

As you read, consider the following questions:

1. When does the author predict that China will become a democracy?
2. What reforms has the Chinese government instituted regarding criminals, according to Rowen?
3. In the author's view, what is the "worldwide—and Asian—norm" regarding the relationship between economic prosperity and political freedom?

Excerpted from "The Short March," by Henry S. Rowen, *Hoover Digest*, 1997. Reprinted with permission from the author.

When will China become a democracy? The answer is, around 2015.

There are two reasons for this forecast: One is positive changes there; the other is the effect of economic growth on freedoms throughout the world.

Freedom House [a nonprofit organization that promotes democracy and human rights] gives China a political freedom rating of zero: It is a one-party state, there are many "counterrevolutionaries" in prison, people are detained without trial, and there were more than two thousand summary executions in 1994. Nevertheless, China has come far since the disasters of the Great Leap Forward and the Cultural Revolution [two of Communist leader Mao Zedong's efforts to economically and socially transform China], notably in three important areas.

Three Signs of Progress

Grassroots Democracy. The dissolution of the communes left no local governments and thus led to village elections. By the early 1990s, 90 percent of village committees had been elected.

Progress has been ragged. Local cadres resist losing privileges, and nonparty members often experience discrimination. Some assemblies require party membership for candidacy. There is some probable ballot fraud, and officials decide if voters can choose more than one candidate. Nevertheless, the principle of competitive elections has been established. Those who oppose party members are no longer "enemies of the people." The concept of rule by law is accepted, with peasants learning about legal procedures and how to protect their rights.

The Rule of Law. Under communism, law is an instrument of politics. Many Chinese now, however, hold that government should observe its own rules. Values consistent with Western ideals of equality, justice, and legality—and also with ancient Chinese ideals—are expressed widely, and some are now embodied in legislation. Officials recognize that a market economy and foreign investment need stable and fair rules.

Contributing to the demand for law is the weakness of the state, with massive corruption, illegal businesses run by government agencies, and theft of government assets. Most basic is the party being outside the jurisdiction of the ordinary courts. Other problems are enforcing decisions in civil proceedings, the immunity of military enterprises, and bribery of judges.

The People's Congress is rewriting the criminal laws. Defendants are not to be presumed guilty and will have their own lawyers. The police no longer will be able to hold people without charge. Doubtless these laws will often be violated, but their passage is significant.

The Mass Media. Economic liberalizing had the unintended effect of liberalizing the mass media. Financial losses led to publications being forced into the market, first books and then newspapers. In Xinhau's bookstores in 1979, the huge state media empire had 95 percent of the market; by 1988, its share had shrunk to 33 percent. Nonparty newspapers gained at the expense of party ones.

The government once controlled the electronic and film media, but falling demand led to unprofitable operations being privatized and to some government stations adopting live coverage of stories, talk shows, call-in programs, twenty-four-hour broadcasting, and celebrity interviews of once-silenced liberal intellectuals.

Television sets, radios, cassette players, and VCRs became widely owned. By the early 1990s, eighty thousand institutions had faxes, there were sixteen thousand satellite ground stations, and, despite legal prohibition, 4.5 million home satellite dishes were operating.

Once a totalitarian regime opts for market reforms, it loses much of its control of information. Today there is self-censorship, as well as government censorship, but there have not been criminal proceedings against journalists—with the exception of some accused of selling state secrets to Hong Kong newspapers—for several years.

Doubtless there will be more cycles of liberalization and repression, but the level of information freedom is rising inexorably.

The Growth of Democracy in Asia

When Taiwan was at China's current economic level, there were local elections, bosses became more responsible, and non-Kuomintang people became active in politics. [The Kuomintang is the dominant political party in Taiwan.] In 1973, its Freedom House democracy score was twenty-five (on a scale of zero to one hundred). This opening process then moved up the political ladder to where Taiwan has had its first, and free, presidential election.

The Myth of China as a Totalitarian State

For all its imperfections and injustices, China today is freer than it has been at any time in the last five decades. About 40,000 Chinese students are now enrolled in tertiary U.S. educational institutions; during the Soviet Union's entire 70-year history, it never sent that many students to the United States. In 1965, there were 12 television and 93 radio stations in China; today, PLA [People's Liberation Army] receiving dishes are sold illegally to citizens who pull in satellite TV. The Internet is growing by leaps and bounds. Newspapers and magazines have become not just more numerous but far more diverse and autonomous. In 1978, the state controlled more than 90 percent of GNP [gross national product]; in 1996, that number was about 45 percent and falling. The state now employs only 18 percent of the work force, compared with more than 90 percent in 1978 (including peasants in communes at that time). In September 1997, at the Fifteenth Party Congress, the concept of "public" ownership was morphed from Marx's concept into "public" in the sense of "initial public offering" of stock. While under Mao the concept of the individual suing the state for damages was inconceivable, it now happens increasingly often.

David M. Lampton, *Foreign Policy*, Spring 1998.

The path in South Korea was different, but the endpoint was the same. Elections were held under Park Chung Hee, but the ruling party determined outcomes. South Korea's 1974 freedom rating was thirty-three—but by 1995 it was eighty-four.

South Korea and Taiwan are two examples of a worldwide—and Asian—norm. By and large, the richer the country, the freer (oil riches aside). If China keeps growing rapidly, its per capita gross domestic product will be seven thousand dollars in 2015, the level at which democracy everywhere has become stabilized. China's freedom rating then is likely to be similar to Taiwan's in 1984 (thirty-three) and on the verge of becoming much higher.

Of course, sustained growth is not guaranteed: the regime might crack down again or conflict with Taiwan or others could become an obstacle. Or China might just be different. . . .

Implications for the United States

It is a good thing that China became rich, for it will benefit the American economy in the process and a richer China will become more democratic. This will not necessarily make it easier to deal with, but experience has shown that democracies are less-dangerous interlocutors for other democracies than are dictatorships. Washington should therefore stop holding trade relations hostage to an array of current political disputes. The United States should instead make most-favored-nation status for China permanent and impose no extra obstacles to its admission to the World Trade Organization (WTO). Our economic interests need to be pressed on the many trade issues in contention, but it is much better to address them in the WTO forum than in the current, highly politicized, bilateral tit-for-tat manner in which we have been engaged in recent years. . . .

We should not assume that China will inevitably become a threat to U.S. interests. We have a common interest with China in seeing its people prosper and at peace, in dealing with environmental problems, and in coping with the dangers associated with the spread of weapons capable of mass destruction. This common agenda would be better advanced if China were a member of the various organizations that make the rules on such matters. Nonetheless, American criticism of China's human rights violations should and will continue, but it should not be linked to trade issues. Our criticisms will have increasing resonance inside a China with a better-educated and informed population that has access to greatly improved telecommunications, a China that is growing freer year by year. . . .

Americans sustained the cold war with the Soviet Union for forty-five years until victory came. The prospect of a twenty-year (more or less) effort to help the Chinese people become free—while helping Taiwan retain its freedoms—is much less daunting. There may be trouble with China during its passage to democracy—or even after—but the odds should go down as it becomes more prosperous. We should do nothing to interfere with that process.

> "*For the foreseeable future China will be governed by top-down authoritarian leadership with tight controls on political dissent.*"

China Is Not Becoming More Democratic

James R. Lilley

In the following viewpoint, James R. Lilley, a former U.S. ambassador to China and director of the American Institute in Taiwan, rejects the idea that China is becoming a democratic nation. Free market forces do seem to be pushing China toward Western-style capitalism, he admits, but he points out that China has a long history of authoritarian rule and that previous attempts by foreigners to influence China's development have been met with violence. Lilley concludes that the Chinese people are more concerned with economic progress than with meeting westerners' hopes for a political transformation in China.

As you read, consider the following questions:
1. What historical examples does the author give of instances in which foreigners attempted to influence China, and failed?
2. What is the "overriding slogan for most Chinese today," in the author's opinion?
3. What forces will influence the next generation of Chinese leaders, in Lilley's view?

Reprinted from "Is China Becoming More Democratic?" by James R. Lilley, *American Enterprise*, July/August 1998. Reprinted with permission from *American Enterprise*.

W ill China transform itself into a Western-style democracy? Can the United States do anything to encourage this? Before answering, consider Yale professor Jonathan Spence's book *To Change China*. Spence describes the failed attempts of foreigners, from the Jesuit Matteo Ricci in the seventeenth century to General George Marshall in the twentieth, to impose solutions on an imperfect China. In all cases, China was influenced but did not convert.

A History of Violence

Christianity came to a weakened China in force after the Opium War of 1840. The result was not a Christian China but the Taiping Rebellion, which killed 20 million Chinese and was led by an epileptic who believed he was the brother of Jesus Christ. Marxism came to China in 1921 when the Communist party of China was founded in Shanghai. The result was not a new socialist China in the Stalin model but the Great Leap Forward of 1959, when Chairman Mao hoped to propel China into the advanced stage of Communism. Instead, 40 million Chinese died—most of them starved to death in failed communes. When free market forces were introduced into Communist China in 1978 by Deng Xiaoping, the result was not an evolving democracy but the massacre at Tiananmen Square in 1989.

In short, when outsiders apply their standards to China and try to introduce new systems quickly or forcefully, what occurs is never quite what was planned. Tragedy can ensue. China does alter course, but in a Chinese way.

Today, free market forces are pushing back the state in nearly all sectors of China's economy. Christianity has never been stronger. Yet China is still ruled by a single Communist party backed by a powerful military and bureaucracy which will not give up a monopoly political power.

A History of Authoritarian Rule

Authoritarian rule in China has lasted for 4,000 years. An emperor has historically ruled from the center with the support of a massive bureaucracy. There are long traditions of violence and suppression, of conformity and enforced collectivized living, of ruler worship and obedience. A political timidity, not easily uprooted, lies at the center of Chinese society.

Moreover, today no organized opposition is permitted to root in labor unions, civic organizations, youth groups, or other bodies which could challenge the regime. The Chinese have lived for ages with this phenomenon. And the fact that today's authoritarian state can deliver a better material life to most Chinese, while also providing a nationalist vision of a restored Greater China, works to keep forces of political change in check.

Still No Free Elections in China

Back in 1987, when China's leaders began an experiment of holding elections at the village level, Deng Xiaoping predicted that it would be 50 years before China held nationwide elections. At the rate things are going, that may have been optimistic. . . .

It might seem logical that these elections would inevitably exert upward pressure, and lead to voting for leaders in counties or towns. But the village elections are no herald of real democracy. They are held without exception under the control of the local Communist Party organization. Even in the cases where voters have a genuine choice between two candidates, both have arrived on the ballot only after being deemed acceptable to the higher authorities.

China has undergone sweeping economic and social change in the 1990's, but remarkably little political change. The people have gained an enormous amount of personal freedom—to choose where they work, where they live and how they spend free time—without gaining any real say in how their national political leaders are chosen. For now, political power resides firmly in the hands of a small group of self-selected men.

Seth Faison, *New York Times*, March 29, 1998.

The overriding slogan for most Chinese today is "Make money, not politics." Attempts to go outside the political system to try to change it can end in death and destruction. Can the system change from within? There have been village elections that have taken on a democratic tinge. There is unquestionably more mobility in society, more openness, and thousands of commercial decisions made daily with no reference to Communist ideology or control.

Democracy Is Secondary to Prosperity

Looking at the dramatic changes that have swept China over the last 70 years, a Western observer can easily be forgiven for predicting that the next stage will be a form of democracy based on rising incomes and middle-class expectations. To support this, dramatic Chinese heroes appear: Wei Jingsheng says there must be a fifth modernization—democracy. Fang Li Zhi, whom I harbored for 13 months when I was U.S. Ambassador to China, says democracy is an historic inevitability based on the principles of physics. Exiled Chinese writers sketch what we want to see: a China of freer speech, democratic elections, and separation of powers.

A new generation of achievement-oriented leaders will soon take charge in China. They will be influenced by Western ways, especially technology, management techniques, and rule of law. But the primary concern of the Chinese will be to grow strong, prosperous, and respected in Asia and elsewhere. Their fears will be chaos, fragmentation, and foreign intervention. Democracy will be important but secondary.

I expect that for the foreseeable future China will be governed by top-down authoritarian leadership with tight controls on political dissent. Economic success and military modernization have given the strong-arm leaders internal legitimacy and world respect. Changes will come to China for pragmatic reasons, but they will be kept within bounds, with no challenges to centralized one-party domination being tolerated.

I expect that although 25 years from now China will look a lot different, the prevailing dynasty will not be ready to fall.

"The [Chinese] Government's poor human rights record deteriorated markedly throughout [1999], as the Government intensified efforts to suppress dissent."

Human Rights Abuses in China Are Widespread

U.S. Department of State

The following viewpoint is excerpted from the U.S. Department of State's *1999 Country Reports on Human Rights Practices*. In it, the State Department lists the human rights violations that occurred in China in 1999, as well as the slow progress that China has made in the area. The authors maintain that the Chinese government routinely arrests, imprison, tortures, and executes individuals who are perceived to be threats to the Communist Party. Chinese citizens do not enjoy freedom of the press or freedom of religion, according to the report. Although the Chinese government has made some efforts to reform its legal system and institute local elections, the report notes that in general, China's political atmosphere remains extremely oppressive.

As you read, consider the following questions:

1. According to the authors, what political party and what spiritual movement were the two main targets of government crackdowns against dissent in 1999?
2. What anniversary was the Chinese government concerned might be used by political dissidents to stage organized protests?
3. What types of persecution and harassment does the report say the Chinese government uses against religious groups?

Excerpted from *1999 Country Reports on Human Rights Practices*, by the U.S. Department of State, February 25, 2000.

The People's Republic of China (PRC) is an authoritarian state in which the Chinese Communist Party (CCP) is the paramount source of power. At the national and regional levels, Party members hold almost all top government, police, and military positions. Ultimate authority rests with members of the Politburo. Leaders stress the need to maintain stability and social order and are committed to perpetuating the rule of the CCP and its hierarchy. Citizens lack both the freedom peacefully to express opposition to the Party-led political system and the right to change their national leaders or form of government. Socialism continues to provide the theoretical underpinning of Chinese politics, but Marxist ideology has given way to economic pragmatism in recent years, and economic decentralization has increased the authority of regional officials. The Party's authority rests primarily on the Government's ability to maintain social stability, appeals to nationalism and patriotism, Party control of personnel and the security apparatus, and the continued improvement in the living standards of most of the country's 1.27 billion citizens. The Constitution provides for an independent judiciary; however, in practice, the Government and the CCP, at both the central and local levels, frequently interfere in the judicial process, and decisions in a number of high profile political cases are directed by the Government and the CCP.

The security apparatus is made up of the Ministries of State Security and Public Security, the People's Armed Police, the People's Liberation Army, and the state judicial, procuratorial, and penal systems. Security policy and personnel were responsible for numerous human rights abuses. . . .

Political Dissidents Are Imprisoned

The Government's poor human rights record deteriorated markedly throughout the year, as the Government intensified efforts to suppress dissent, particularly organized dissent. A crackdown against a fledgling opposition party, which began in the fall of 1998, broadened and intensified during the year. By year's end, almost all of the key leaders of the China Democracy Party (CDP) were serving long prison terms or were in custody without formal charges, and only a

71

handful of dissidents nationwide dared to remain active publicly. Tens of thousands of members of the Falun Gong spiritual movement were detained after the movement was banned in July; several leaders of the movement were sentenced to long prison terms in late December and hundreds of others were sentenced administratively to reeducation through labor in the fall. Late in the year, according to some reports, the Government started confining some Falun Gong adherents to psychiatric hospitals. The Government continued to commit widespread and well-documented human rights abuses, in violation of internationally accepted norms. These abuses stemmed from the authorities' extremely limited tolerance of public dissent aimed at the Government, fear of unrest, and the limited scope or inadequate implementation of laws protecting basic freedoms. The Constitution and laws provide for fundamental human rights; however, these protections often are ignored in practice. Abuses included instances of extrajudicial killings, torture and mistreatment of prisoners, forced confessions, arbitrary arrest and detention, lengthy incommunicado detention, and denial of due process. Prison conditions at most facilities remained harsh. In many cases, particularly in sensitive political cases, the judicial system denies criminal defendants basic legal safeguards and due process because authorities attach higher priority to maintaining public order and suppressing political opposition than to enforcing legal norms. The Government infringed on citizens' privacy rights. The Government tightened restrictions on freedom of speech and of the press, and increased controls on the Internet; self-censorship by journalists also increased. The Government severely restricted freedom of assembly, and continued to restrict freedom of association. The Government continued to restrict freedom of religion, and intensified controls on some unregistered churches. The Government continued to restrict freedom of movement. The Government does not permit independent domestic nongovernmental organizations (NGOs) to monitor publicly human rights conditions. Violence against women, including coercive family planning practices—which sometimes include forced abortion and forced sterilization; prostitution; discrimination against women; trafficking in women and children; abuse of children; and discrimination against the disabled and minorities are all problems. The Government continued to restrict tightly worker rights, and forced labor in prison facilities remains a serious problem. Child labor persists. Particularly serious human rights abuses persisted in some minority areas, especially in Tibet and Xinjiang, where restrictions on religion and other fundamental freedoms intensified.

Beginning in the spring, Communist Party leaders moved quickly to suppress what they believed to be organized challenges that threatened national stability and Communist Party authority. In the weeks before the 10th anniversary of the June 4 Tiananmen massacre, the Government also moved systematically against political dissidents across the country, detaining and formally arresting scores of activists in cities and provinces nationwide and thwarting any attempts to commemorate the sensitive anniversary. Authorities in particular targeted the CDP, which had already had three of its leaders sentenced to lengthy prison terms in December 1998. Beginning in May, dozens of CDP members were arrested in a widening crackdown and more of the group's leaders were convicted of subversion and sentenced to long prison terms in closed trials that flagrantly violated due process. Others were kept detained for long periods without charge. In one August week alone, CDP members Liu Xianbin, She Wanbao, Zha Jianguo, and Gao Hongming were sentenced to prison terms of 13, 12, 9, and 8 years, respectively. Dissidents also were rounded up in large numbers before the October 1 National Day celebrations. In addition, the press reported that the Government rounded up 100,000 or more persons and sent them out of Beijing under the custody and repatriation regulations prior to the October 1 National Day celebrations, to ensure order.

Government Control of the Press

Control and manipulation of the press by the Government for political purposes increased during the year. After authorities moved at the end of 1998 to close a number of newspapers and fire several editors, a more cautious atmosphere in general pervaded the press and publishing industries during the year. As part of its crackdown against the popular Falun Gong spiritual movement, the Government employed every element of the state-controlled media to conduct a nationwide anti-Falun Gong propaganda campaign reminiscent of the campaigns against the democracy movement that followed the Tiananmen massacre of 1989. The press continued to report on cases of corruption and abuse of power by some local officials.

Lack of Religious Freedom

Unapproved religious groups, including Protestant and Catholic groups, continued to experience varying degrees of official interference, repression, and persecution. The Government continued to enforce 1994 State Council regulations requiring all places of religious activity to register with the Government and come under the supervision of official, "patriotic" religious organizations. There were significant differences from region to region, and even locality to locality, in the attitudes of government officials toward religion. In some areas, authorities guided by national policy made strong efforts to control the activities of unapproved Catholic and Protestant churches; religious services were broken up and church leaders or adherents were harassed, and, at times, fined, detained, beaten, and tortured. At year's end, some remained in prison because of their religious activities. In other regions, registered and unregistered churches were treated similarly by the authorities. Citizens worshiping in officially sanctioned churches, mosques, and temples reported little or no day-to-day interference by the Government. The number of religious adherents in many churches, both registered and unregistered, continued to grow at a rapid pace. The Government launched a crackdown against the Falun Gong spiritual movement in July. Tens of thousands of Falun Gong members were reported detained in outdoor stadiums and forced to sign statements disavowing Falun Gong before being released; according to official sources, practitioners of Falun Gong had 35,000 confrontations with police between late July and the end of October. A number of practitioners were detained multiple times. An unknown number of members who refuse to recant their beliefs remain detained; others are serving prison or reeducation-through-labor sentences. An intensive proatheism, "antisuperstition" media campaign also accompanied the suppression of Falun Gong. In October, new legislation banning cults was passed. Adherents of some unregistered religious groups reported that these new laws are used against them.

Tony Auth. Copyright © 1998 by Universal Press Syndicate. Reprinted with permission from Universal Press Syndicate.

Although the Government denies that it holds political or religious prisoners, and argues that all those in prison are legitimately serving sentences for crimes under the law, an unknown number of persons, estimated at several thousand, are detained in violation of international human rights instruments for peacefully expressing their political, religious, or social views. Persons detained at times during the year included political activists who tried to register an opposition party; leaders of a national house church movement; organizers of political discussion groups that exceeded what the Government deemed to be the permissible level of dissent; and members of the Falun Gong movement. Some minority groups, particularly Tibetan Buddhists and Muslim Uighurs, came under increasing pressure as the Government clamped down on dissent and "separatist" activities. In Tibet the

Government expanded and intensified its continuing "patriotic education campaign" aimed at controlling the monasteries and expelling supporters of the Dalai Lama. In Xinjiang authorities tightened restrictions on fundamental freedoms in an effort to control independence groups. . . .

Some Positive Trends

During the year, the Government continued efforts to reform the legal system and to disseminate information about new legislation. Initiatives to improve the transparency and accountability of the judicial and legal systems continued. The Government also expanded efforts to educate lawyers, judges, prosecutors, and the public on the provisions of new laws. A number of statutes passed in recent years—e.g., the Administrative Litigation Law, the Lawyers Law, the State Compensation Law, the Prison Law, the Criminal Law, and the Criminal Procedure Law—if enforced effectively hold the potential to enhance citizens' rights. The revised Criminal Procedure Law, which came into effect in 1997, provided for the defendant's right to legal counsel, an active legal defense, and other rights of criminal defendants recognized in international human rights instruments. If fully implemented, this law would bring criminal laws closer toward compliance with international norms. However, enforcement of the new statute is poor, and the law routinely is violated in the cases of political dissidents.

Despite intensified suppression of organized dissent, some positive trends continued. Nongovernmental-level village committee elections proceeded, giving citizens choices about grassroots representatives, as well as introducing the principle of democratic elections. Additional experiments with higher level township elections were conducted without fanfare (or official approval by the central Government). Social groups with economic resources at their disposal continued to play an increasing role in community life. As many as 8.9 million citizens had access to the Internet, although the Government increased its efforts to try to control the content of material available on the Internet. Most average citizens went about their daily lives without significant interference from the Government, enjoying looser economic controls, increased access to outside sources of information, greater room for individual choice, and more diversity in cultural life. However, authorities significantly stepped up efforts to suppress those perceived to be a threat to government power or to national stability, and citizens who sought to express openly dissenting political and religious views continued to live in an environment filled with repression.

4

"The majority of Chinese today prefer social order and stability to freedom."

The United States Overemphasizes Human Rights Abuses in China

Ming Wan

In the following viewpoint, Ming Wan argues that, while the state of human rights in China is poor according to Western standards, the West fails to realize that the average Chinese person does not place that much importance on human rights. The Chinese government's official position is that human rights concerns are sometimes outweighed by the need to maintain political stability by suppressing dissent. Wan argues that public opinion in China also supports stability over freedom. Wan concludes that the United States should stop trying to force its values on the Chinese people, and instead let them develop their own views on democracy and human rights. Ming Wan is an assistant professor of public and international affairs at George Mason University.

As you read, consider the following questions:

1. What view is encompassed by the term "developmental authoritarianism," as stated by the author?
2. According to the opinion survey cited by Wan, what percent of Chinese polled agreed that they "would rather live in an orderly society than in a freer society which is prone to disruption"?
3. What evidence is there that the Chinese people support their government, according to Wan?

Excerpted from "Chinese Opinion on Human Rights," by Ming Wan, *Orbis*, Summer 1998. Reprinted with permission from Elsevier Science.

No issue in Sino-American relations invokes as much passion as human rights. At stake, however, are much more than moral concerns and hurt national feelings. To many Americans, the Chinese government is ultimately untrustworthy on all issues because it is undemocratic. To the Chinese government, U.S. human rights pressure seems designed to compromise its legitimacy, thereby casting an altogether different light on what might otherwise be "normal" disputes in international relations over such issues as trade, arms sales, and intellectual property rights.

Ignoring China's "Silent Majority"

Washington's diplomatic pressure has produced little progress on human rights in China, and, indeed, human rights advocacy rarely yields immediate results whenever target governments, especially major powers such as China, put up strong resistance. But Americans' lack of understanding about political and social developments in China has also aggravated the situation and led to misjudgments about timing and degrees of pressure. What has been missing in the public debate in the United States is the Chinese voice. Western attention has focused mainly on Beijing's declared policies and Chinese dissidents' opinions. Hence, U.S. policy prescriptions and media commentaries are too often based on the simplistic view of a repressive Communist government ruthlessly frustrating a society of aspiring democrats, as represented by courageous human rights fighters like Wei Jingsheng. But does anyone know what China's "silent majority" thinks? The evidence suggests that the Chinese majority is in fact quite vocal in its own circles, expressing strong opinions about China and U.S. policy toward it.

Decision makers and other observers should know and care about the views of ordinary Chinese since what is being debated in the United States is not conventional diplomacy but rather a campaign to pressure the Chinese government according to America's notion of how a "civilized" member of the international community should behave. That implies an attempt to reweave the very fabric of Chinese political and social life, hence the receptivity of Chinese society is central to the wisdom and feasibility of such a U.S. approach.

One basic assumption in much American writing about China is that its repressive government is standing in the way of progress and is thus "on the wrong side of history." That assumption is what legitimizes U.S. pressure on China. Since the end of the Cold War, Washington has displayed increasing confidence in the inevitable triumph of human rights and democracy and can point to some evidence to substantiate such a view. The 1989 Tiananmen incident illustrated, on prime time TV, the extent of discontent within China, and Chinese dissidents strike an American audience as sympathetic spokesmen for democracy. But what if such impressionary evidence does not reflect the norm? What if Chinese society as a whole does not share the same fundamental values as American society? Should the United States still exert pressure on China over human rights and democracy? . . .

The Chinese Government's Official Stance

Government views on human rights and democracy are best represented by President Jiang Zemin. His 1997 state visit to the United States provided a rare opportunity for the outside world to hear his personal views on these issues. Jiang presented himself as an open-minded leader, but he differed sharply with his American hosts on human rights issues. The spontaneous exchange between Jiang and President Clinton at a joint press conference on October 29 illustrated this in striking fashion. Responding to a reporter's question about the Tiananmen incident, Jiang claimed that "the Communist Party of China and the Chinese government have long drawn the correct conclusion on this political disturbance, and facts have also proved that if a country with an over 1.2 billion population does not enjoy social and political stability, it cannot possibly have the situation of reform and opening up that we are having today." Clinton responded that the Chinese government "is on the wrong side of history" on this issue. Jiang also held spirited debates over human rights with U.S. congressional leaders.

Jiang's statements were severely criticized by American human rights groups, the media, and congressional leaders. But his remarks reflect the dominant view in the Chinese government. What has emerged as a convergence point for most government and party agencies is "developmental authoritarianism," which calls special attention to China's *guoqing* or state conditions. According to this view, stability is critical for achieving economic development as the country's primary objective.

"Looks like we're going nowhere fast!"

Lurie's World Copyright © 1995 Worldwide Copyright by Cartoonews International Syndicate, N.Y.C., USA. Reprinted with permission.

The government agencies not centrally involved with human rights have more pressing issues at hand: to promote economic reform, avoid political turmoil, raise living standards for their districts or working units, and promote the careers of their officials. My own field research in China and discussions with Chinese cadres visiting the United States have repeatedly confirmed that developmentalism prevalis among Chinese officials. As a typical example, a deputy head of a major state enterprise from a northern city concluded during his first visit to the United States that the "beautiful country"—the literal translation of the Chinese name for the United States—is blessed with natural resources, giving it leeway to allow greater personal freedom than poorly endowed China. Chinese should focus on improving their living standards and therefore they need stability. . . .

China's "Silent Majority" Speaks

It is difficult to know precisely the opinions of ordinary Chinese in the absence of systematic national polls to allow time-series and cross-section analyses of public opinion. It is possible, however, to sketch a portrait of Chinese society based on the occasional opinion polls conducted in China in recent years, as well as on the views expressed in interviews, seminars, conferences, and Internet groups. This rough portrait displays some interesting features about Chinese society.

First, the majority of Chinese today prefer social order and stability to freedom. Based on a survey conducted in Beijing in December 1995, Yang Zhong, Jie Chen, and John M. Scheb II found that 33.8 percent of those polled agreed that they "would rather live in an orderly society than in a freer society which is prone to disruption" and another 61.8 percent *strongly* agreed with the statement. Only 3.6 percent and 1.6 percent disagreed or strongly disagreed. To be sure, the survey question was based on the premise that more freedom risks instability, which is not necessarily so, although the government clearly emphasizes such a connection to its own advantage. The phrasing of the question, therefore, may well have skewed the results in the direction of support for order over freedom. However, the notion that freedom may lead to instability is persuasive to many ordinary Chinese, given their collective experience with past political experiments and turmoil. The answers to this question suggest widespread worries among ordinary citizens about political change that promises greater freedom but may also undermine stability. Chinese are generally cautious toward political and economic change. The extraordinary energy exhibited during the 1989 Tiananmen incident illustrated the potential of Chinese society for political change, but the broad support shown for student protesters stemmed more from a desire to end official corruption than for democracy. Under normal circumstances, most Chinese are not active politically. In addition, many Chinese consider the fate of the former Soviet Union and draw a negative conclusion about the wisdom of promoting democracy at all costs.

Secondly, Chinese political culture still exhibits some undemocratic attributes that may create problems if the country were to undergo democratization now. Based on a national survey conducted in China in 1990, Andrew J. Nathan and Tianjian Shi identified potential difficulties in Chinese political culture for immediate democratization. Compared with citizens in more advanced nations, Chinese show lower levels of awareness of the government's impact on their daily lives, lower expectation of fair treatment from the government, and lower tolerance of ideas with which they disagree. Although educated Chinese score higher in perceived government impact and political tolerance than their less educated countrymen, [Nathan and Shi write that] they are still "substantially less likely to hold democratic orientations than people of the same educational levels elsewhere." The Chinese are thus caught in a sort of "Catch-22": they cannot acquire the attributes necessary for democratization in the absence of democratic experience itself.

Thirdly, Chinese are becoming more individualistic, the young especially so. Chinese are also increasingly aware of their rights, property rights in particular. A poll conducted in 1994 in Beijing indicated that when presented with "stories" of rights violations, an absolute majority of people were aware of their rights, with urban residents more informed than rural residents. In fact, Chinese people are more concerned about economic rights than social and political rights. This pattern is illustrated by a project entitled *Social Development and Protection of Civil Rights in China* conducted by a Chinese research team from 1992 to 1995. Its nationwide survey showed that while 50 to 60 percent of respondents would be highly resentful if the fruits of their labor were seized by government cadres, almost one-third of those polled would exhibit no resentment if someone entered their house without permission. Chinese are even less assertive about their political rights: only 15 percent of those polled had considerable or strong resentment about having no opportunity to voice their opinions on policy and law.

Economic Rights Will Lead to Political and Civil Rights

If China replicates the experience of Taiwan and South Korea, a greater awareness of property rights will, in the end, lead to a greater awareness of political and civil rights. But, based on the evidence to date, this connection has yet to be made in China. In fact, according to the 1992–95 national survey mentioned earlier, between one-third and one-half of respondents answer that the rights to personal safety, to election and dismissal of cadres, and humane treatment in confinement are granted by the state. And only 1 to 3 percent think people are *born* with these rights. Since the start of the reform, almost all new rights have been granted to the people by the state and only a few civil rights initiatives have come from below.

A powerful combination of aversion to political instability and awareness of economic interests and rights provides a fertile ground for developmentalist and instrumentalist views of human rights, now shared by the government and most of the society. According to these views, China's paramount objective should be economic growth, political stability is essential to assure China's continued success in development, and democracy may not suit China's current needs given the country's unique and difficult *guoqing*. This perspective is reinforced by general satisfaction among Chinese with their rising living standards, the country's rising status on the world stage, and their wish to see a powerful and prosperous China.

The prevalence of such views among ordinary Chinese explains why human rights and democracy continue to be perceived as foreign concepts remote from daily life. Given such a social and political environment in China, it is not surprising that U.S. pressure has contributed not to growing demands for democracy, but to rising nationalist sentiments within the Chinese society.

Indeed, the most striking trend in China today is the strong political conservatism combined with nationalist emotions, even among intellectuals, to which U.S. pressure has arguably contributed. Although misperceptions to the effect that the United States is conspiring to destabilize China may be fanciful, they nonetheless condition policy debates and decisions in China and should be taken seriously by American analysts.

Contrary to the perception in the West that the Chinese government is an illegitimate regime that has survived solely by coercion, there is now considerable public support in

China for the government. Jie Chen, Yang Zhong, and Jan William Hillard found strong popular support for the regime in a survey conducted in Beijing in December 1995. What is more, that popular support appears to have grown. In a nationwide survey conducted by a team of American-trained Chinese scholars between 1986 and 1987, there was only "moderate" support for the political regime, even though support for the country was strong. It is difficult to draw definite conclusions based on the two surveys, which followed different procedures. But the findings confirm rather than contradict the impression one gets that there is stronger public support for the government now than in the mid-1980s. . . .

Implications for Sino-American Relations

This discussion of Chinese perspectives on human rights and democracy has important implications for Sino-American relations. While U.S. policymakers must continue to bow to Americans' moral concerns and their own political interests, they also must recognize how concerned, or relatively unconcerned, a majority of Chinese are about human rights and democracy at a given time. As Chinese society evolves, a dialogue between the two nations is possible and can prove productive. Certainly when Chinese citizens are ready to push for greater democracy and human rights, they will seek inspiration both from Chinese tradition and the experience of existing democratic nations, with the United States as one of the shining examples. However, it is important to recognize that although American concerns and the concerns of Chinese society somewhat overlapped from 1989 to 1990, there is at present a chill. If China's "silent majority" does not respond to Western pressure, then interventionist diplomacy is unwise and counterproductive: unwise because any pressure that does not strike a sympathetic chord with ordinary Chinese will fail, and counterproductive because human rights pressure only contributes to rising nationalism in China. The Chinese have the same right to evolve morally and politically, on their own terms and at their own pace, as the United States has done. And the one thing the United States cannot do is to hasten the process through its own impositions in an attempt "to save China from the Chinese."

"If China needs to have a population policy, it should be based on volunteerism and education, not coercion and intimidation."

China's One-Child Policy Violates Human Rights

Harry Wu

In the 1970s, China began to implement a nationwide family planning policy—called the "one-child policy" because under it couples are strongly discouraged from having more than one child. In the following viewpoint, Harry Wu asserts that the Chinese government routinely forces sterilization or abortion on women who attempt to have a second child. Wu concludes that China's one-child policy is unnecessary and that the ways in which it is enforced constitute serious abuses of governmental authority. Harry Wu is executive director of the Laogai Research Foundation, an organization that collects information about forced labor camps and other human rights violations in China.

As you read, consider the following questions:
1. What four policies do "planned-birth supervision teams" use against violators of the one-child policy, according to Gao as paraphrased by Wu?
2. According to Wu, what type of information is included in the "synopsis of planned-birth report" that workers such as Gao must file on a monthly basis?
3. What two arguments does the author list to refute the idea that overpopulation has kept China from developing as a nation?

Excerpted from "Forced Abortion and Sterilization: The View from the Inside," by Harry Wu, July 1998. Reprinted with permission from the author. Article available at www.laogai.org.

It has been over twenty years since the People's Republic of China, which has 22% of the world's population, began implementing its population control policy, or planned birth policy, in Mainland China. In the years following the 1949 victory of the Communist Party in the PRC, Communist leader Mao Zedong promoted population growth, regarding a large population as an asset for both production and security. In the most recent decades, as the focus of the Chinese government has shifted towards economic development, the Communist government has taken to blaming the cultural traditions of its own people for the population explosion. The need to promote development and combat the tradition of large families became justifications for one of the most barbaric abuses of government power ever revealed: the infamous "one child" policy.

Since 1979 when the population control policy was first implemented, it has been a top-down system of control: the central government establishes general policy guidelines, and local governments institute and enforce specific directives and regulations to meet these guidelines. In addition to the original one-child policy itself, the Marriage Law of 1980 requires the practice of family planning. The law encourages the policy of late marriage and late birth, and sets the minimum marriage age at 22 years of age for men and 20 years of age for women. Provincial regulations enacted in the eighties established artificial quotas, which planned birth cadres were to enforce strictly. Leaders in Jiangxi, Yunnan, Fujian, and Shaanxi provinces, for example, received orders to strictly limit the number of births in excess of their authorized targets by forcing women to have abortion, euphemistically referred to as "taking remedial measures."

In May of 1991, the Chinese Communist Party Central Committee enacted the "Decision to Intensify Planned-Birth Work and Strictly Control Population Growth." This policy paper contains provisions suggesting the use of IUD's, sterilization, and pregnancy termination in some circumstances. In all, the policy aims to create a greater uniformity between central and provincial family planning and laws. While there have been alternate tightenings and relaxations of the policy, the evidence brought to light at the June 10, 1998 hearing before the House Subcommittee on International Operations and Human Rights revealed that the coercive practice first implemented in the eighties persist to this day. Never before has this system been exposed to the world in its entirety. In fact, up until this point, the Chinese government has been internationally applauded for its effective population control efforts. The Chinese government has always insisted that it uses only voluntary methods for controlling the amount of children born into Chinese families. Unfortunately, evidence repeatedly contradicts this empty assertion.

China's Population Policy Exposed

Gao Xiao Duan, a former cadre in a planned-birth office in Yonghe Town in Fujian Province, testified before the House of Representatives Subcommittee on International Operations and Human Rights on June 10, 1998, and exposed the system of oppression before a packed hearing room. Gao, still a Chinese citizen, was employed as an administrator at the Yonghe town planned-birth [office], where her job was to "work out and implement concrete measures pursuant to the documents of the Central Committee of the Chinese Communist Party, and the State Council on planned-birth." In other words, she was to carry out the dictates of the communist regime in accordance with the "one child" policy. Her day-to-day duties were as follows:

• To establish a computer data bank of all women of child-bearing age in the town (10,000+ women), including their dates of birth, marriages, children, contraceptive ring insertions, pregnancies, abortions, child-bearing capabilities, menstruation schedule, etc.

• To issue "birth allowance" certificates to women who meet the policy and regulations of the central and provincial planned-birth committees, and are therefore allowed to give birth to children. Without this certificate, women are not allowed to give birth to children. Should a woman be found to be pregnant without a certificate, abortion surgery is performed immediately, regardless of how many months she is pregnant.

• To issue "birth-not-allowed notices." Such notices are sent to couples when the data concludes that they do not meet the requirements of the policy, and are therefore not allowed to give birth. Such notices are made public, and the purpose of this is to make it known to everyone that the couple is in violation of the policy, therefore facilitating supervision of the couple.

Harsh Enforcement of the One-Child Policy

In the mid-'80s, according to Chinese government statistics, birth control surgeries—abortions, sterilizations, and IUD insertions—were running at a rate of 30 million a year. Numbers for more recent years are unavailable; the government, embarrassed by reports of coercion and female infanticide, has refused to release them. Many—if not most—of these operations are performed on women whose "consent" has been wrung from them by an escalating series of threats and punishments. "You will be fired from your job unless you comply" is a common form of arm-twisting.

China's population control officials have been known to abort and sterilize women by force, a fact which comes through sometimes in odd ways. In October 1997, for instance, Beijing proudly unveiled its latest "family planning" weapon: A mobile abortion unit. The occasion was the 24th International Population Conference, hosted by Beijing and attended by 1,400 delegates from around the world. A white van rolled up to the conference hall as official Zhou Zhengxiang explained to the delegates China's plans to make 600 of these units to travel around the countryside. The rear door was thrown open for inspection and the delegates were invited to inspect its equipment. They saw a bed, suction pumps, and—a body clamp. *A body clamp.*

Steven Mosher, *American Enterprise*, July/August 1998.

• To issue "birth control measures implementation notices." According to their specific data, every woman of child-bearing age is notified that she has to have contraceptive device reliability and pregnancy examinations when necessary. Should she fail to present herself in a timely manner for these examinations, she will not only be forced to pay a monetary penalty, but the supervision team will apprehend her and force her to have such examinations.

• To impose monetary penalties on those who violate the provincial regulations. Should they refuse to pay these penalties, the supervision team members will apprehend and detain them as long as they do not pay.

• The municipal planned-birth committee often sends random "go-to-the-countryside cadres" to villages, for fear that local cadres could cooperate with villagers, or that a local backlash would develop against the cadres who conscientiously carry out their duties. . . .

• Whenever the planned-birth office calls for organizing "planned-birth supervision teams," the town head and communist party committee secretary will immediately order all organizations—public security, court, finance, economy—to select cadres and organize them into teams. They are then sent to villages, either for routine door-to-door checking or for punishing of local violators. Supervision teams are makeshift, and to avoid leaks, cadres do not know the village to which they will be sent until the last minute. Planned-birth supervision teams usually exercise night raids, encircling suspected households with lightning speed. Should they fail to apprehend a woman violator, they may take her husband, brother(s), or parent(s) in lieu of the woman herself, and detain them in the planned-birth office's detention room until the woman surrenders. They then would perform a sterilization or abortion surgery on the woman violator.

Use of Force and Coercion

Gao also outlined several policies that are carried out in the wake of "planned-birth supervision":

• House dismantling. No document explicitly allows dismantling of a violator's house. To the best of her knowledge, however, this practice not only exists in Fujian Province, but in rural areas of other provinces as well.

• Apprehending and detaining violators. Most planned-birth offices in Fujian Province's rural areas have their own detention facilities. In her town, the facility is right next door to her office. It has one room for males and one room for females, each with a capacity of about 25–30 people. To arrest and detain violators, the planned-birth office does NOT need any consent by judicial or public security institutions, because their actions are independent of those organizations. . . .

• Sterilization. The proportion of women sterilized after giving birth is extraordinarily high. Sterilization can be replaced with a "joint pledge," with 5 guarantors jointly pledging that the woman in [the] case shall not be pregnant again. Much of the time, however, this kind of arrangement is impossible, because five people are unlikely to be willing to take on the liability of having to guarantee that a woman will not become pregnant. It is important to remember that if she does, by some chance, become pregnant, they are responsible for her actions, too.

• Abortion. According to government regulations, abortion for a pregnancy under 3 months is deemed "artificial abortion," and if the pregnancy exceeds three months, it is called "induced delivery." In her town, an average of 10–15 abortion surgeries are performed *monthly*, and of those surgeries, one third are for pregnancies exceeding 3 months.

Every month her town prepares a report, the "synopsis of planned-birth report." It enumerates in great detail the amount of births, issuing of birth-allowed certificates, and implementation of birth-control measures in Yonghe Town. Following its completion, it is submitted to the planned-birth committee. For instance, in January-September 1996, of all the women of child-bearing age with 1 child, 1,633 underwent device-insertion surgeries, or underwent subcutaneous-device-insertion surgeries, and 207 underwent sterilization surgeries; of women of child-bearing age with 2 children, 3,889 underwent sterilization surgeries, 167 underwent device-insertion surgeries, and 10 took birth-control medications (among the group with 2 children, of the 186 women who had 2 daughters, 170 were sterilized). In January–September 1996, a total of *757 surgeries* in *five categories* were performed. They included: 256 sterilization surgeries (35 for two daughters), 386 device-insertion surgeries (23 cervical ring insertions), 3 subcutaneous-device-insertions, 41 artificial abortion surgeries, and 71 induced delivery surgeries. In the first half of the year of 1997, a total of *389 surgeries* in 5 categories were performed. They included: 101 sterilization surgeries (12 for two daughters), 27 induced delivery surgeries, 228 device-insertion surgeries, and 33 artificial abortion surgeries. Gao's office had to submit all of this data to the municipal planned-birth committee monthly and annually so that it could be kept on file.

Personal Tales of Sorrow

Gao and her husband were married in 1983, and gave birth to their daughter one year later. Despite their desire to have more children, they were not allowed to give birth to a second child due to the planned-birth policy. She and her husband wanted another child very badly, and in late 1993, they adopted a boy in Northeast China in Harbin, a province in northeast China. They had no choice but to keep him in someone else's home. For fear of being informed against by others in the town, the child never referred to Gao as "mama" in the presence of outsiders. Whenever government agencies conducted door-to-door checks, her son had to hide elsewhere.

Her elder sister and her elder brother's wife have only two daughters each. Both of them were sterilized, their health ruined, making it impossible for them to ever live or work normally.

During her 14-year tenure in the planned-birth office, she witnessed how many men and women were persecuted by the Chinese communist government for violating its "planned-birth policy." Many women were crippled for life, and many of them were victims of mental disorders as a result of their unwanted abortions. Many families were ruined or destroyed. Gao, with tears streaming down her face, told during her testimony of how her conscience was always gnawing at her heart.

She vividly recalled how she once led her subordinates to Yinglin Town Hospital to check on births. She found that two women in Zhoukeng Town had extra-plan births. In a move approved by the head of the town, she led a planned-birth supervision team composed of a dozen cadres and public security agents. Sledge hammers and heavy crowbars in hand, they went to Zhoukeng Town, and dismantled the women's houses. Unable to apprehend the women in the case, they took their mothers and detained them in the planned-birth office's detention facility. It was not until a month and a half later that the women surrendered themselves to the planned-birth office, where they were quickly sterilized and monetary penalties were imposed. Gao spoke at length about how she thought she was conscientiously implementing the policy of the "dear Party," and that she was just being an exemplary cadre.

Once Gao found a woman who was nine months pregnant, but did not have a birth-allowed certificate. According to the policy, she was forced to undergo an abortion surgery. In the operation room, she saw the aborted child's lips sucking, its limbs stretching. A physician injected poison into its skull, the child died, and it was thrown into the trash can. As she testified, "To help a tyrant do evils" was not what she wanted. . . .

The Population Policy Analyzed

I testified at the hearing to show how the Chinese policy is truly a top-down system. For many years I have collected many stories about the tragic experiences of people who are affected by the planned-birth policy. Their personal experiences may be more emotionally shocking, but I want to explain China's internal documents that I have collected over the years. The basic arguments for China's population policy are:

• China's living and land resources are limited, which tremendously impedes its development, added to which is population growth. To become a prosperous nation, China must control its population growth.

• Limited economic resources and overpopulation cause disruption of education, the environment, health services, and negatively affect quality of life issues in China.

In short, the Chinese government wishes people, especially Chinese citizens, to believe that overpopulation makes China a backward nation, and that controlling it will allow them to develop as a nation. Such a point of view is preposterous, and is countered by the following two observations:

• Certain nations such as Japan have even more limited per capita living resources than China, but are nevertheless extraordinarily prosperous.

• Is it not the lack of a rational social and economic system that retarded China's development in the years following the rise of the Communist Party? For several years after the 1949 Communist victory, China's economy did in fact make great strides—without a population control policy. Economic backwardness resumed because of failed communist economic experiments. After economic reforms that started in the late 70's under Deng, the economy has again improved. The economic advances that China has made in the last two decades should be attributed to economic reforms rather than to the strict population policy. This is not to say that population control had nothing to do with the economic growth China has experienced, but it is a well-known observation that as economies prosper, fertility rates decrease. This explains why fertility rates have declined more naturally in the urban areas of China; the relatively economically progressive cities do not have to be as coercive with the policy, because the couples who live there today do not wish to have as many children as their rural counterparts.

It is the communist political and economic system that makes it difficult to develop China's economy, and is the fundamental reason for the contradiction between an exploding population and a retarded economy. Therefore, the fundamental way to solve China's population problem is to change its irrational political and economic system. Planned-birth targets every family, every woman. . . .

Whether you are pro-choice or pro-life is irrelevant in this situation; this is an issue of humanity. If China needs to have a population policy, it should be based on volunteerism and education, not coercion and intimidation. To give birth and plan your family is a fundamental human right, and should be deprived from no one.

"China's promotion of family planning has created . . . the population conditions for safeguarding the survival and development of China."

China's One-Child Policy Does Not Violate Human Rights

Information Office of the State Council of the People's Republic of China

The following viewpoint is excerpted from an official document published by the Information Office of the State Council of the People's Republic of China. China's policy is that family planning is a necessary response to the problem of overpopulation and that it benefits the Chinese people in a variety of ways by ensuring that China's finite resources are not spread too thin. Moreover, the authors contend that China's family planning is consistent with human rights principles, reasoning that an individual's right to reproduce is outweighed by the harms associated with unrestricted population growth.

As you read, consider the following questions:
1. In what year did China first begin to promote family planning?
2. According to the Chinese government's official statistics, as of 1994, what percent of married women of child-bearing age had volunteered to have only one child?
3. According to the authors, what problems would ensue if "the reproductive freedom of couples and individuals are unduly emphasized"?

Excerpted with permission from "Family Planning in China," by the Information Office of the State Council of the People's Republic of China, August 1995. Article available at www.china.org.cn/English/index.html.

China's reform and opening to the outside world as well as its economic development have created a favourable socioeconomic environment for family planning, while the achievements of family planning have in turn created a favourable population environment for the continuous development of the economy, the improvement of the people's living standards as well as the overall progress of society.

Slowing Population Growth

Family planning has effectively checked the trend of over-rapid population growth. In the 15 years from the founding of the People's Republic to 1964, China's population increased from 500 million to 700 million, and on average 7.5 years were needed for the population to increase by 100 million. The 1964-74 period was one of high-speed growth where China's population increased from 700 million to 900 million in ten years, and the time needed for the population to increase by 100 million was shortened to five years. In 1973, China began to promote family planning throughout the country. China's population increased from 900 million to 1.2 billion in the period from 1973 to February 1995, and the time needed for the population to increase by 100 million was again lengthened to around seven years. China has been through the third post-1949 peak period of births from the beginning of the 1990s, the community of women in their prime of fertility (aged 20 to 29) has exceeded 100 million each year on average, and such a huge child-bearing community has a great birth potential still. But, because China's current population and family planning programmes and policies have won understanding and support from the people, the fertility level of the population has steadily reduced and the trend of overrapid population growth has been effectively checked along with the country's economic and social development. Compared with 1970, in 1994 the birth rate dropped from 33.43 per thousand to 17.7 per thousand; the natural growth rate, from 25.83 per thousand to 11.21 per thousand; and the total fertility rate of women, from 5.81 to around 2. Now, China's urban population has basically accomplished the change-over to the population reproduction pattern characterized by low birth rate, low death rate and low growth; and the rural population is currently in this process of change-over. According to statistics supplied by the United Nations, China's population growth rate has already been markedly lower than the average level of other developing countries. According to calculation by experts, if China had not implemented family planning but had all along kept the birth rate at the level of the early 1970s, its population would possibly have passed the 1.5 billion mark by now. Over the past two decades and more, China's promotion of family planning has created a population environment conducive to reform and opening to the outside world and socioeconomic development as well as the population conditions for safeguarding the survival and development of China.

Encouraging Smaller Families

Family planning has promoted the change of people's concepts regarding marriage, birth and family. Since the implementation of the policy of family planning in China, profound changes have been taking place in people's concepts of marriage, birth and family along with the reform and opening to the outside world as well as socio-economic development; the traditional ideas of "early marriage and early births," "more children, greater happiness," and "looking up on men and down on women" are being discarded by more and more people at the child-bearing ages. Late marriage and late births, fewer and healthier births, viewing male and female children as the same, establishing happy, perfect and harmonious small families and seeking a modern, scientific and civilized way of life have become an irresistible trend of the times. The rate of early marriage for women has come down and their average age at first marriage has gone up. In 1992, the proportion of women entering first marriage before the age of 20 dropped to 12.9 percent of the total number of first-marriage women. In 1970, women's average age at first marriage was 20.2 years, while in 1993 it was 22.67 years, up 2.47 years. The family size has become gradually smaller and the nuclear family is becoming the major form of modern Chinese families. According to China's fourth national census, the average size of families in 1990 was 3.96 persons,

0.88 person less than the 4.84 persons in 1971. The major reason for the reduction of family size is a reduction in the number of births. Compared with 1970, of the babies born in 1993 the first-birth rate and second-birth rate increased from 20.7 percent and 17.1 percent to 61.3 percent and 27.5 percent respectively, and the multiple-birth rate dropped from 62.2 percent to 11.2 percent. By 1994, a total of 46.76 million couples had volunteered to give birth to only one child throughout the country, accounting for 20.3 percent of the total married women at child-bearing age. At the current level of economic development and living standards in China, the reduction of family size and fewer children to support have obviously reduced the economic burden and the burden of family chores on the families and improved their quality of life. . . .

Improving Quality of Life

Family planning has promoted the improvement of the quality of the Chinese population in terms of . . . health as well as the overall development of the people. China's family planning has always included the two aspects of controlling the population size and improving the population quality in terms of education and health. While making efforts to control the population at an appropriate size, the Chinese government has devoted great attention to developing educational, medical and other services in order to continuously improve the quality of the population in terms of education and health. Prior to 1949, the mortality rate was as high as 20 per thousand, while by the end of the 1970s it had dropped to below 7 per thousand. From 1949 to 1990, the life expectancy rose from 35 years to 68.55 years—66.84 years for males and 70.47 years for females, making China a country where the life expectancy increased the most rapidly. Great improvements have been witnessed in the basic facilities for public health in China. Throughout the country, the average number of hospital beds for every 10,000 people increased from 13.3 in 1970 to 23.6 in 1994, and the average number of professional medical workers and technical workers in the field of medicine for every 10,000 people went up from 17.5 in 1970 to 35 in 1994. The incidence of various contagious diseases has markedly dropped. The diet of urban and rural people throughout the country has greatly improved, the per-capita daily calorie intake has reached 2,600 Kcal. and that of protein has reached 75 grammes, having reached or approaching the world average levels. Health care for women and children has continuously expanded. Now, family planning as well as maternity and child care networks have been basically formed in China's urban and rural areas. The mortality rate for babies dropped from 200 per thousand prior to the founding of the People's Republic to 35 per thousand in 1990, the death rate of expectant and new mothers was 94.7 per 100,000, and the rate of planned immunity for new-born babies reached 85 percent. The major indexes of people's medical care and health have already far outstripped countries at the same level of economic development, and the gap with the developed countries is being gradually narrowed. . . .

Improving the Status of Women

Family planning has further liberated the female productive forces and helped improve the status of women. Family planning in China has extricated women from frequent births after marriage and the heavy family burden, further liberated and expanded the social productive forces latent in women, and provided them with more opportunities to learn science and general knowledge and take part in economic and social development activities, hence greatly promoted the improvement of the Chinese women's status in economic and social affairs as well as in their families.

The employment rate of women has steadily increased and sphere of employment has continuously expanded. By the end of 1992, the number of female staff and workers had reached 56 million in China, accounting for 38 percent of the national total of staff and workers and representing a 24.1 percent increase over the 45 million in 1985. In the 1979–88 period, the growth rate of employment for urban women had always been higher than that for men, with the average annual increase standing at 4.9 percent, 1.27 percentage point higher than the average annual increase of all staff and workers countrywide. The overwhelming majority of Chinese women are located in the countryside, and they are the major force of the agricultural production and diversified economy in the country. They are that part of the population to benefit most from the policy of family planning. . . .

China Is on the Right Track

Certainly we must move ahead with family planning, modernization, and improving the education and status of women. . . . [However,] those programs must be supplemented by non-coercive incentives to reduce desired family size in almost all nations to not more than two children. . . .

Possible incentives vary widely, and include tax and financial incentives, and those for schooling, housing, jobs, pensions and late marriages, among others. . . .

China and Singapore are examples of countries where incentives have resulted in unprecedented and rapid declines in fertility. In China, from 1965–1970 to 1975–1980, fertility fell by more than three births per woman, largely due to its national program of incentives and disincentives.

There were undoubtedly elements of coercion in the Chinese program, and those elements have been widely, and rightly, denounced. Without either condoning or defending those coercive practices, we should, however, endeavor to understand the magnitude of the problem China faces. Chinese authorities point out that they are struggling to feed 22 percent of the world's population on just seven percent of its arable land. They maintain that the staggering pressure of China's huge and still growing population on a land of scarce resources made tough controls unavoidable.

The point here is that a program of incentives need not be coercive, and is not, as some might argue, inherently so. Because China's program was in some respects flawed, does not mean that the entire concept should be abandoned.

Negative Population Growth, "Position Paper on the Cairo Conference on Population and Development," August 1994.

Family planning has provided women with more opportunities to receive education and is conducive to raising their educational qualities. At present, the average schooling for adult women in China's urban areas totals 9.97 years. Of these women, those who have received education of senior middle school or higher account for 56.3 percent; those who have received junior middle school education account for 33.3 percent; those who have received primary school education account for 8.3 percent; and those who are illiterate and semi-illiterate account for only 2.1 percent. For the previous generation, however, those with senior middle school education and higher account for only 9.1 percent; those with junior middle school education, 11.1 percent; those with primary school education, 24.5 percent; and illiterates and semi-illiterates, 55.3 percent. For adult women in the rural areas, those with senior middle school education or higher make up 8.9 percent; those with junior middle school education, 26.6 percent; those with primary school education, 27.9 percent; and illiterates and semi-illiterates, 36.6 percent. For the previous generation, those with senior middle school education or higher account for only 0.5 percent; those with junior middle school education, 1.9 percent; those with primary school education, 9.0 percent; and illiterates and semi-illiterates, 88.6 percent.

Eradicating Poverty

Family planning has accelerated the process of eradicating poverty in rural China. In China's poor areas, economic and cultural backwardness and too many births often interact as both cause and effect. The Chinese government has taken an important step in giving support to the development of poor areas to alleviate poverty by promoting family planning, holding population growth under control, and raising the life quality of the population in those areas. Since 1978, the state has adopted a series of measures to make those living below the poverty line drop from 250 million to 70 million in 1995. The Chinese government has combined the solution of the problem of the portion of society living under the poverty level with family planning to free families from the vicious cycle of "the poorer they are, the more children they give birth to, and the more children they give birth to, the poorer they become." In this respect, marked achievements have been obtained. In the communities that have extricated themselves from poverty, farming households that have implemented family planning are often in a clearly advantageous position.

The positive impact produced by family planning on Chinese society is wide and profound. With the passing of time, the benefits of family planning, for the people and for posterity, are bound to be more apparent. . . .

Family Planning Is in Accordance with Human Rights

Family planning in China is pursued in complete accordance with the relevant principles and human rights requirements designated by the international community. China's family planning policies and programmes combine citizens' rights and duties, joining the interests of the individual with those of society. These conform to the basic principles outlined at the various international population conferences and have been established on the basis of the relationship of interpersonal interests under socialism. Never in any country are rights and duties absolute, but rather, they are relative. There are no duties apart from rights, or rights apart from duties. When there is conflict between social needs and individual interests, a means has to be sought to mediate it. This is something that the government of every sovereign country is doing. As China has a large population, the Chinese government has to limit the number of births of its citizens. This is a duty incumbent on each citizen as it serves the purpose of making the whole society and whole nation prosperous, and it is not proceeding from the private interest of some individuals. This is wholly justifiable and entirely consistent with the moral concepts of Chinese society. To talk about citizens' rights and duties out of reality in an abstract and absolute way does not hold water either in China or in any other country. In a heavily populated developing country like China, if the reproductive freedom of couples and individuals are unduly emphasized at the expense of their responsibilities to their families, children and societal interests in matters of child bearing, indiscriminate reproduction and unlimited population growth will inevitably ensue. The interests of the majority of the people, including those of new-born infants, will be seriously harmed.

We should see that in China, especially in rural, backward and remote areas, there is a gap between the desire for childbirth of some couples of child-bearing age and the demand of the present family planning policy, and shortcomings of one kind or another are unavoidable in family planning work. However, as the family planning policy fundamentally conforms to the interests of the majority of the Chinese people and, during its actual implementation, the actual difficulties and reasonable demands of some people have been taken into consideration and the legal rights and interests of the citizens are strongly protected, the family planning policy has won understanding and recognition from the broad masses of the people. Through long period of practice, the Chinese people have realized more and more deeply from their practical interests that family planning is a cause that benefits the nation and the people, and they have increasingly come to understand and support this cause. After unremitting efforts, including drawing useful experience from other countries, the management level and service quality of China's family planning programme have continually been improved and the shortcomings and problems in its actual work has been remarkably reduced. We believe that all those who do not seek to hold prejudice will respect this basic fact.

> "*If China's appalling behavior does not warrant trade sanctions, what nation's does?*"

Economic Sanctions Should Be Imposed on China

William Saunders

William Saunders is foreign policy and human rights counsel to the Family Research Council, a nonprofit organization that promotes traditional values. In the following viewpoint, Saunders calls on U.S. policymakers to institute economic sanctions against China in order to pressure it into curbing its human rights abuses. He favors revoking China's "Normal Trade Relations" status (the name was changed from "Most Favored Nation" status in 1997), under which trade between the United States and China is free of protective tariffs and other barriers. Saunders maintains that economic sanctions are an effective alternative to military action as a means of achieving foreign policy goals.

As you read, consider the following questions:

1. What argument did advocates of "Most Favored Nation" status for China make in 1997, according to the author?
2. In the author's opinion, why is China not a "free-trader"?
3. In Saunders's view, what fundamental principle does China lack?

Reprinted from "What's 'Normal' About Free Trade with China?" by William Saunders, *Perspective*, 1999. Reprinted with permission from the author.

On June 3, [1999] President Clinton with callous audacity commemorated the eve of the 10th anniversary of the Tiananmen Square massacre by asking Congress once again to reward China with renewal of its Normal Trade Relations (NTR) status. A strange thing to do, considering that there's nothing "normal" about U.S. relations with China. What is normal about conducting business as usual with a Chinese regime that lies to its people about NATO's accidental embassy bombing and virtually holds our ambassador hostage in the U.S. embassy by staging riots around him?

The last time America seriously debated China's trade status, [in 1997], it went by another name, Most Favored Nation (MFN). Changing MFN's name can't change the fact that there is less reason for normal trade with China today than there was in 1997. Problems then identified by opponents of MFN renewal have worsened, and new problems have been discovered.

Human Rights Abuses Continue

Advocates of MFN renewal in 1997 argued that trade with China would introduce the "virus of freedom" that could spread to other segments of Chinese society, leading to religious and political freedoms as well. Unfortunately, the opposite has happened. As the State Department announced in its annual Human Rights Report in February [1999], the Chinese government's human rights record has "deteriorated sharply."

Members of "unofficial" churches continue to be jailed, and their churches destroyed. The group Human Rights in China reported that 7,140 Protestant house church leaders were arrested in October and November [1999] alone. One of them, Cheing Meiying, was whipped and beaten so badly that she suffered brain damage. . . .

Opposition political leaders have been sentenced to harsh prison terms in "trials" little different from the infamous Communist show trials in Eastern Europe in the 1950s. Xu Wenli, Qin Yongmin and Wang Youcai were sentenced to 13, 12 and 11 years respectively for trying to organize the new China Democratic Party.

China's policy of coerced abortions and sterilization continues. Before being deported from Australia to China, Zhu Qingping, eight months pregnant, was promised she would not be forced to abort her child. When she arrived, however, she was forced into a car and taken to the hospital, where her child was aborted against her will.

China's Bullying Tactics

The Chinese regime continues to build its military strength aggressively and ignore weapons proliferation agreements. Since the last MFN debate, we have learned that China has systematically stolen some of our most sensitive and sophisticated military secrets. China's oppression of Tibet continues unabated, and its saber-rattling toward Taiwan has become more serious. Our growing trade deficit with China is financing its military by funneling hard currency into the many companies owned by the People's Liberation Army.

The Chinese regime's hatred and deception of America is more evident than ever. It ludicrously denies its military espionage and obvious attempts to influence U.S. elections and policies through illegal campaign contributions. During the riots it orchestrated outside the U.S. embassy in Beijing, the Chinese president refused to take President Clinton's calls. China also canceled bilateral talks on weapons proliferation and human rights.

China's contrived temper tantrum is a plain attempt to bully the United States into approval of NTR renewal for China and of its admission to the World Trade Organization (WTO). Yet China is not even a free trader. Despite Chinese promises to complete economic reforms by 1997, one-third of the nation's economy is still state-owned. China also continues to violate its promise to respect intellectual property rights. Chinese trade officials reneged on WTO promises Zhu Rongji made during his U.S. visit within days of his making them. Worried that true free-market reforms would promote what they fear most—political instability—China's totalitarians have insisted on receiving favorable terms throughout WTO negotiations. Such concessions would seriously undermine the integrity of WTO rules.

The fundamental problem is that China lacks a principle that Western democracies take for granted—the rule of law.

Innocent "protesters" and ordinary Chinese citizens are not the only people who need and deserve rule of law in China, though. U.S. businesses operating in China cannot long prosper without it either. In order to plan effectively, business needs the predictability that the rule of law ensures. Yet, in China's totalitarian system the government changes the "rules" secretly and capriciously, and enforces them unevenly and unfairly.

Free Trade Has Not Improved China's Human Rights Record

In 1994, when President Clinton formally separated China's "most favored nation" trading status from its human rights record, he insisted that this did not diminish our commitment to pursuing a vigorous human rights policy. The Administration even went so far as to claim that economic growth and liberalization in China, fueled by increased trade with the United States, would actually promote political liberalization.

Five years down the road these assurances have proved to be empty rhetoric. [In the fall of 1998], the Chinese authorities undertook the toughest crackdown on dissidents since the Tiananmen Square massacre a decade ago. The State Department's own human rights report, released in February [1999], acknowledged that "China's human rights record has deteriorated sharply over the past year." As that record has worsened, though, the 1994 "de-linkage" has turned into complete disassociation. Human rights and trade are no longer parts of the same overall policy package but are proceeding on completely separate tracks.

Paul Wellstone, *New York Times*, April 5, 1999.

Shortsightedly, many in the American business community favor NTR and WTO for China. We must weigh their views carefully. Perhaps the most disturbing aspect of the Chinese espionage scandal has been the apparent willingness of some U.S. businesses to transfer "dual use" (particularly missile) technology to the Chinese, in violation of U.S. law. We must not allow commercial interests alone to set U.S. foreign policy. Human rights, national security, and common sense all have a role to play.

Nearly everyone agrees there should be "engagement" of some sort with China, but at what price? If China's appalling behavior does not warrant trade sanctions, what nation's does? And if we practically never apply economic sanctions against any regime, what is left in our foreign policy portfolio beyond military options?

It is incumbent upon advocates of unfettered trade with China to propose some other effective mechanism for pressuring its regime to address the worsening problems we have discerned since 1997. Otherwise, NTR renewal should be denied until China has instituted meaningful economic reforms and demonstrated a serious commitment to human rights and the rule of law. What we have been doing is not working.

"Economic sanctions . . . are not an effective tool to promote human rights."

Economic Sanctions Should Not Be Imposed on China

David Dreier

Congressman David Dreier is a California Republican and chairman of the House Rules Committee. In the following viewpoint, he argues that China should continue to receive "Most Favored Nation" status (now known as "Normal Trade Relations" status). Economic sanctions are an ineffective means of promoting human rights in other countries, he maintains. China's economic reforms have resulted in greater prosperity and more freedom; economic sanctions would only undermine that prosperity and cause China to backslide into more repression. Moreover, if the United States were to impose economic sanctions on China, the action could draw the two nations into a disastrous cold war.

As you read, consider the following questions:

1. How does Dreier describe "one of the great truths of the twentieth century"?
2. What other nations does the author say have overcome dictatorship and political repression by adopting market-based economic reforms?
3. In what nations does the author say that U.S.-imposed economic sanctions have led to greater economic and political repression?

Fostering freedom and human rights around the world is a universal foreign-policy goal in Congress. That was the case in 1989, when I joined nearly a dozen of my colleagues, Democrats and Republicans, in a march to the front door of the Chinese Embassy to protest the brutal massacre of student protesters in Beijing's Tiananmen Square. It remains a bipartisan priority today because support for freedom and democracy is part and parcel of what it means to be American. . . .

In looking at conditions in China during the last 20 years, the path to democracy of numerous countries around the globe and the effectiveness of unilateral economic sanctions to improve human rights for people living under the boot of other repressive regimes, it becomes unmistakably clear that such sanctions will not improve human rights in China. If anything, economic sanctions will set back the cause of freedom.

Achieving greater human freedom in China is an important priority if for no other reason than the fact that one-fifth of the human race lives in that vast country. Today, the Chinese people lack individual rights, political freedom and freedom of speech, religion, association and the press. Even the most basic human freedom of childbearing is regulated by the authoritarian national government.

China Has Made Substantial Progress

When looking at repression in China, however, I am reminded of the ancient saying that, in the land of the blind, the one-eyed man is king. It does no good to evaluate progress toward freedom in China by comparing it with the United States or any other democracy. Instead, a historical perspective is needed.

While China offers a 4,000-year story of political repression, some of its bleakest days have come in the last generation. More than 60 million Chinese starved to death during Mao Tse-tung's disastrous Great Leap Forward, and another million were murdered by the Communists during the international isolation of Mao's Cultural Revolution. The Chinese were scarred by those brutal events, and no one wants to return to the terror of economic calamity and starvation.

[In 1997] Stapelton Roy, the former American ambassador to China, put the current conditions in China in the following perspective: "If you look at the 150 years of modern Chinese history you can't avoid the conclusion that the last 15 years are the best 15 years in China's modern history. And of those 15 years, the last two years are the best in terms of prosperity, individual choice, access to outside information, freedom of movement within the country and stable domestic conditions."

Today, the Chinese economy is the fastest growing in the world. While many Chinese remain poor peasants, few go hungry, and hundreds of millions of Chinese have seen their lives substantially improved through economic reform. Many enjoy greater material wealth and a greater degree of personal economic freedom. Market reform is the single most powerful force for positive change in China in this century and possibly in the country's long history. The recent economic progress, which significantly has improved living conditions in China, is a profound moral victory. Fostering further positive change is a moral imperative as well.

As reported in the March 4 [1997] *New York Times*, Zhu Wenjun, a woman living outside Shanghai, has seen her life improve dramatically due to economic reform. Zhu, 45, quit a teaching job that paid $25 a month to work for a company that exports toys and garments that pays $360 a month. "It used to be that when you became a teacher, you were a teacher for life," Zhu was quoted as saying. "Now you can switch jobs. Now I am talking with people overseas and thinking about economic issues."

Economic Reform from Within China, Not Sanctions from Without

Economic reform in China has helped to lift hundreds of millions of hardworking people from desperate poverty, giving them choices and opportunities never available before. Hundreds of millions of Chinese have access to information and contact with Western values through technologies spreading across the country, thanks to economic reform and the growth it created. This is a tremendous victory for human freedom.

Americans are justified in their outrage about the Chinese government's policy methods of population control. This

111

has led many Chinese families to abort female babies with the hope of having a son. Here again, moral outrage and economic sanctions will not be enough to end this violation of basic human rights.

The *New York Times* reported another encouraging story from inside China that shows how economic reform undermines repression, including China's one-child policy. Ye Xiuying is a 26-year-old woman who runs a small clock shop in Dongguan, a small town in Guangdong province. Through her own entrepreneurial spirit and energy, she rose from a $35-per-month factory worker to running her own business and earning up to $1,200 a month. Along with buying a home and looking forward to traveling to the United States, Ye used $1,800 to pay the one-time government fine so she could have a second child.

The Problem with Sanctions

A free-market approach to human rights policy does not mean an attitude of indifference toward human rights abuses. Using slave labor or political prisoners and compelling very young children to compete in international markets are wrong. But blanket restrictions, such as the denial of most-favored-nation (MFN) trading status or the use of sanctions not directly targeting the wrongdoers, should be avoided. The problem is that even limited actions are very difficult to enforce and unlikely to bring about political change in an authoritarian regime.

James A. Dorn, *Freeman*, May 1997.

The hopeful stories of Zhu and Ye have been repeated many, many times across China during the last 15 years. That is why Nicholas Kristoff, former *New York Times* Beijing bureau chief, said, "Talk to Chinese peasants, workers and intellectuals and on one subject you get virtual unanimity: 'Don't curb trade.'"

The Chinese are learning firsthand one of the great truths of the late 20th century: Market-oriented reforms promote private enterprise, which encourages trade, which creates wealth, which improves living standards, which undermines political repression.

While full political freedom for the Chinese may be decades away, other hopeful signs of change exist. Today, 500 million Chinese farmers experience local democracy, voting in competitive village elections in which winners are not Communist candidates. The Chinese government also is recognizing that the rule of law is a necessary underpinning of a true market economy. Furthermore, the Chinese media, while strictly censored, increasingly are outside the control of the party and the state. In particular, the spread of communications technology throughout China, including telephones, fax machines, computers, the Internet, satellites and television, is weakening the state's grip on information.

The evidence that market reforms are the main engine driving improved human rights in China is mirrored around the globe. South Korea, Taiwan, Chile and Argentina all broke the chains of authoritarian dictatorship and political repression during the last 25 years primarily because their respective governments adopted market-based economic reforms. As a result, each country grew wealthier and more open and each eventually evolved into democracies.

Economic Sanctions Do Not Promote Freedom

The cause of human freedom advanced in those instances in which the United States did not employ economic sanctions against dictatorships. In contrast, decades of American economic sanctions against Iran, Iraq, Libya and Cuba, while merited on national-security grounds, only have led to greater economic and political repression.

The real-world failure of economic sanctions to result in human-rights gains has left proponents of sanctions groping for new arguments. The argument du jour is that China is our next Cold War adversary, and since the United States used trade sanctions against the Soviet Union in a successful Cold War campaign, the same strategy should be applied to China.

This line of thinking is fundamentally flawed. A Cold War with China is unthinkable absent the support of our international allies, and the simple reality is that a Cold War strategy would garner no support. During the Cold War with the Soviet Union, the world's democracies by and large saw an aggressive military opponent bent on undermining democracy around the world. Today, China is not viewed as a similar threat to democracy nor to international peace and security. China's neighbors, while concerned with that country's evolution as a major economic and political power, do not advocate Cold War–style confrontation. The United States' closest allies in Asia—Japan, Korea, Australia and Thailand—strongly oppose economic warfare with China. They see economic reform as a condition of peace and security in the region.

The unwillingness of our allies to join us in a crusade against China largely is based on the fact that China has not earned international enmity. The Soviet Union conquered its neighbors in Eastern Europe and imposed puppet regimes on previously independent countries. They invaded Afghanistan and instigated violent insurrections throughout Africa, Latin America and Asia. The Soviet Union earned the Ronald Reagan label, "evil empire." Chinese foreign policy, even with its distressing proliferation policies, is in a different league altogether.

The national-security rationale for anti-China sanctions is as weak as the human-rights arguments. Just as economic engagement consistently has proved to be the best human-rights policy, Cold War–style economic sanctions are national-security fool's gold. Imposing economic sanctions on China would throw away the real progress of the last 15 years and send 1.2 billion people to the darkest days of Maoism. When Reagan called on Mikhail Gorbachev to "tear down this wall" [the Berlin Wall], he demanded freedom for Eastern Europeans to mingle with the West—just the opposite of the spirit of trade sanctions against China, which attempt to erect new walls around the Chinese people.

Economic sanctions, especially when imposed unilaterally, are not an effective tool to promote human rights. Economic sanctions against China would undermine the market reforms that have been the single most powerful force for positive change in that country. They could shatter the hopes and dreams of 20 percent of the human race seeking to rise above the poverty and oppression that have been staples of Chinese history.

Periodical Bibliography

The following articles have been selected to supplement the diverse views presented in this chapter. Addresses are provided for periodicals not indexed in the *Readers' Guide to Periodical Literature*, the *Alternative Press Index*, the *Social Sciences Index*, or the *Index to Legal Periodicals and Books*.

America	"The People's Republic at 50," October 9, 1999.
Sophie Beach	"Tiananmen Plus Ten," *Nation*, June 14, 1999.
Gwendolyn Dean	"We Must Boycott China's Goods," *Christian Social Action*, January 1998.
Bay Fang	"China Draws a Hard Line," *U.S. News & World Report*, January 24, 2000.
Robert D. Kaplan	"Sometimes, Autocracy Breeds Freedom," *New York Times*, June 28, 1998.
William McGurn	"The Other China," *American Spectator*, July 1999.
Jonathan Mirsky	"Nothing to Celebrate," *New Republic*, October 11, 1999.
Paul Murphy	"Tale of Two Tibets," *World & I*, June 1997. Available from 3400 New York Ave. NE, Washington, DC 20002.
A.M. Rosenthal	"Can We Do Business with China?: Put Principles Before Trade," *Reader's Digest*, October 1998.
Henry S. Rowen	"The Short March: China's Road to Democracy," *National Interest*, Fall 1996. Available from P.O. Box 622, Shrub Oak, NY 10588-0622.
James D. Seymour	"Human Rights, Repression, and 'Stability,'" *Current History*, September 1999.
Xu Wenli	"The Democracy Movement in China," *World & I*, February 1999.
Harry Wu	"The Outlook for China, Human Rights," *Vital Speeches of the Day*, June 15, 1996.

CHAPTER 3

Does China Pose a Threat to the United States?

Chapter Preface

In May 1999, Congress released a report detailing evidence that China had spied on the United States for twenty years. The Cox report, named after Republican Christopher Cox who headed the House committee that released it, claims that Chinese agents stole information about every nuclear weapon currently deployed by the United States and that China could use this information to improve their own nuclear capabilities. Many of the thefts occurred at the Los Alamos National Laboratory in New Mexico, but the report also states that U.S. companies such as Hughes Electronics Corporation may have inadvertently given away some U.S. secrets when they launched satellites aboard Chinese rockets.

Not surprisingly, the nuclear espionage scandal outraged many Americans. Critics of U.S. foreign policy cited the incident as proof that China is seeking to gain a military advantage over the United States. Some politicians, such as House Republican Tom DeLay, also used the incident to question "whether the president and vice president deliberately ignored the reality of Chinese spying and theft because they had ulterior economic and political motives," referring to illegal campaign contributions the Democratic party received from Chinese donors in the 1996 presidential race.

However, some argue that the Cox report provides little evidence for its broad claims of espionage. Stephen L. Schwartz of the *Bulletin of Atomic Scientists* asks, "If China has been diligently swiping our technological secrets for the past 20 years . . . why is it still using military hardware it designed in the 1960s and 1970s?" Others contend that China should not be demonized because of the spy scandal; Michael Klare, professor of peace and world studies at Hampshire College, maintains that "China, like every other country in the world, spies. . . . There is nothing unusually sinister about this."

The Los Alamos spy scandal is just one incident inciting debate over China. The authors in the following chapter consider China's strategic goals and its military capabilities as they consider whether China poses a threat to U.S. interests around the globe.

"There is increasing evidence that a new conflict with an authoritarian regime is in prospect, this time with Communist China."

Conflict Between the United States and China May Be Imminent

Frank J. Gaffney Jr.

In the following viewpoint, Frank J. Gaffney Jr. argues that the Chinese government may have long-term plans that are harmful to the United States and its vital interests. The author claims that, among other things, the People's Republic of China is building up its armed forces, spying on the United States, and establishing relations with American allies and with anti-U.S. countries such as Iraq. Gaffney believes that to prevent future conflict with China, the United States should act now to subvert the Chinese Communist regime while also building up U.S. defensive capabilities in Asia. Gaffney is president of the Center for Security Policy in Washington, D.C.

As you read, consider the following questions:
1. What U.S. vulnerabilities does the author claim China is attempting to exploit through "asymmetric" means?
2. Why is it especially difficult to counter Chinese espionage, in Gaffney's view?
3. What policies of the Clinton-Gore administration does Gaffney believe may have been affected by illegal Chinese campaign contributions?

Reprinted from "Are the United States and China on a Collision Course?" by Frank J. Gaffney Jr., *American Legion Magazine*, March 2000. Reprinted with permission from the author.

The single-most important strategic question of the coming decade is likely to be: Is Communist China determined to harm the United States or its vital interests? The second-most important question is: If so, can conflict between our nations be avoided on terms that are consistent with the American people's security and liberties?

Before examining these important issues, consider this observation about forecasts: There are few inevitabilities in the course of human conduct. Decisions taken—or not taken—at various points along the road can and do shape history. In hindsight, events may appear to be inevitable. But they rarely are.

The trouble is that, when living through a transitional period, we often are unaware of the turning points, of the choices being made. For example, take the period that led up to World War II.

Today we can clearly see evidence that the Nazis and Japanese were pursuing courses that would bring them into conflict with the United States and other Western democracies. We can also see the missed opportunities during the 1930s when different policies on the part of this country, Britain and France might have spared the world the conflagration that followed.

Yet at the time, the democracies were lulled into inaction by the seductive appeal of those who claimed that engaging with the thugs running Germany and Japan on their terms—a practice that came to be known as "appeasement"—would spare the West the tragic costs of another conflict.

This approach was tried again and again in the face of what proved to be insatiable demands by members of the fascist Axis. Feeding the tiger only made it come back for more. Despite the fact that Great Britain and Nazi Germany were each other's largest trading partners, the war came when it suited Hitler.

What Beijing Wants

Unfortunately, I believe there is increasing evidence that a new conflict with an authoritarian regime is in prospect, this time with Communist China. As in the 1930s, this evidence is somewhat obscured by other information—what intelligence experts call "noise." Some of it is genuine. Some of it is misinformation.

The difficulty of understanding which is greatly compounded by the efforts of those, like their counterparts of 60 years ago, who tell us that engagement will prevent conflict, that expanding trade and accommodation of China's demands will ensure that peaceful relations between our two countries are preserved.

In fact, trade and accommodation will not necessarily prevent conflict with the People's Republic of China any more than it caused Hitler to refrain from attacking Britain's allies and, in due course, England herself. China is, after all, not the United States' "strategic partner."

As in the 1930s, we ignore evidence of a coming struggle with China at our peril. If anything will make that conflict inevitable, it will be our failure to address what the PRC is up to and the strategic implications of that behavior and policies that guide it for our vital interests and those of our allies in Asia.

Ominous Trends

Consider the following illustrative list of China's ominous activities. Motivation and likely repercussions of these activities must be separate from the "noise" and addressed effectively.

• *The PRC's ambitious military modernization program:* The Communist Chinese are engaged in what Mao might have called a "Great Leap Forward" in the lethality and power projection capabilities of their armed forces. The purpose of this effort is clear to those guiding the PRC's People's Liberation Army: to neutralize (preferably without a war) and, if necessary, defeat what the PLA's political commissars constantly refer to as "the main enemy"—the United States.

Importantly, this effort is guided by a strategy of Sun Tzu, ancient China's most famous warrior-philosopher. It is not meant to replicate America's mighty military. Rather, it is being guided by a desire to find "asymmetric" means of exploiting our vulnerabilities. These have been identified as including: the United States' dependence on space for communications, navigation and reconnaissance; the susceptibility of our advanced electronic equipment to devastating electromagnetic pulse weapons; the current inability of the U.S. Navy to stop the sort of supersonic, anti-ship missiles China is now acquiring from Russia; and the absence of American defenses against ballistic missiles.

Particularly worrisome is the fact that China is acquiring the capability to exploit these vulnerabilities. Worse yet, this is being done, in no small measure, via technology acquired legally or illegally from the United States as well as through a growing strategic alliance with Russia.

• *Dividing and intimidating U.S. allies in the region:* The Chinese are shrewdly exploiting their North Korean clients' ballistic missile programs (as well as brandishing the PRC's own inventory of offensive missiles). A principal goal is to convince Taiwan, Japan, the Philippines and South Korea that their ally, the United States, is a declining power incapable of defending them, making accommodation with Beijing the only option for containing the threat. China's president, Jiang Zemin, has made the point directly and bluntly in announcing that "Asian values" (code words for authoritarian subordination of the rights of the individual to the good of the masses) are a basis for a "new world order."

• *China's espionage:* In the wake of the . . . spy scandal at Los Alamos, there is a growing awareness of the unprecedented magnitude of PRC efforts to collect classified and other sensitive information in the United States. Notably, Paul Moore, who for many years served as the FBI's top counterintelligence expert for China, has described this effort as massive, comprehensive, patient and deadly. It differs dramatically from the problem posed by Soviet moles and other agents during the Cold War. By exploiting the family ties and sentimental attachment to the motherland of many overseas Chinese, the pool of individuals who can be induced or compelled to gather even seemingly inconsequential data makes the challenge of tracking, to say nothing of counteracting, PRC espionage stupifyingly difficult.

• *China's penetration of our hemisphere:* From Canada to Brazil, Beijing is making steady inroads into the Western hemisphere. Its operations include: drug, alien and arms smuggling operations; replacing the Soviet Union as Cuba's principal international patron; developing military ties with

America's friends like Ecuador and Paraguay; militarily relevant space cooperation with Brazil; introducing PLA combat engineer brigades into Latin America in the name of assisting in infrastructure development; and securing, via a Chinese company with close ties to the PRC's military and intelligence services, effective control of the Panama Canal.

• *The PRC's increasing assertiveness around the Pacific Rim and Asia:* In Pakistan and Myanmar, in Malaysia and waters claimed by the Philippines, Beijing is establishing relationships, bases and intelligence collection facilities that offer China unprecedented opportunities to project its power and influence.

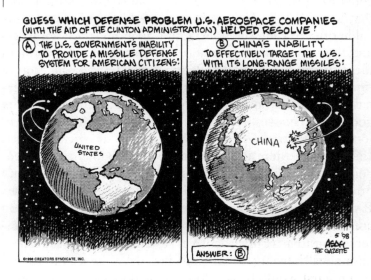

Reprinted with permission from Chuck Asay and Creators Syndicate.

• *Chinese proliferation:* The PRC sees its trade in weapons technology as a powerful vehicle for winning friends and influence with useful rogue states such as Libya, Syria, Iraq, Iran and North Korea. By so doing, the Chinese are greatly exacerbating the power of anti-U.S. forces.

• *Penetration of the U.S. capital markets by PLA and Chinese government-affiliated entities:* These entities are raising billions of dollars from largely unsuspecting American investors via debt and equity offerings. The effect is a "two-fer" for Beijing: It can simultaneously secure vast new quantities of largely non-transparent, undisciplined funds while giving potentially millions of our countrymen a vested interest in the appeasement of China lest their pension funds, life insurance portfolios, mutual funds or other investments be jeopardized.

• *China's penetration of the U.S. political system:* Finally, there is the appearance that illegal Chinese campaign contributions may have shaped the Clinton-Gore administration's policies toward China. Affected areas appear to include: presidential decisions about the transfers of satellite and missile technology; the sale of hugely powerful supercomputers; distancing the United States from its long-time ally, Taiwan; looking the other way on China's human rights violations; and the PRC's accession to the World Trade Organization on terms favorable to Beijing. This behavior is all the more worrisome when it comes against the backdrop of significant internal unrest in China. Will Beijing use external aggression as a pretext for imposing greater control at home and diverting public anger from the government to foreign "barbarians"—a technique known as "social imperialism" often exploited by authoritarian regimes in trouble?

What Can and Should We Do?

If we have the wit to understand these policies for what they are—actual or potential threats to our security and vital interests—there are several things we can do to mitigate, if not eliminate, the danger they pose.

The first would be to adopt a new policy of engagement. This would involve a concerted effort to resist the communist regime and work on bringing about its downfall as Ronald Reagan worked to destroy an earlier "Evil Empire" [the Soviet Union]. Such a policy would brook no further trade subsidies for China and intensify outreach efforts, through Radio Free Asia and other means, to those inside the PRC anxious to bring about its complete transformation to a democratic nation.

The United States should also be focusing on rebuilding our allies' confidence in American power and security guarantees, something sorely lacking today and critically needed if we are to reinvigorate and expand our relations with other democracies in Asia.

A second initiative would reinforce the first by sharing critical defensive capabilities with those in Asia with whom we share democratic values. A top priority, in light of the growing threat posed by Chinese and others' long-range missiles, would be for the United States to build and deploy effective anti-missile defenses for both our forces and allies overseas and for the American people here at home. The way to acquire this capability fastest, most effectively and least expensively is from the sea, by giving the Navy's AEGIS fleet air defense system the ability to shoot down ballistic missiles.

Finally, we must preserve the ultimate guarantor of our security, and that of our allies: America's nuclear deterrent. The Senate's recent rejection of the Comprehensive Test Ban Treaty—which would have denied us the one proven means of assuring the safety, reliability and effectiveness of our arsenal—was a step in the right direction. We must now act to assure those criteria are satisfied for the foreseeable future by conducting periodic underground nuclear tests and taking sensible steps to upgrade our current nuclear inventory.

By making prudent choices, we may not be able to prevent an ultimate conflict with Communist China. But we will be acting to minimize that horrible prospect and to put ourselves in the strongest possible position to deal with it in the event the collision proves unavoidable.

> *"The prospects of world peace, stability and progress will be jeopardized if the current unnecessary rush toward confrontation is not reversed by both [the United States and China]."*

Conflict Between the United States and China Can Be Averted

Henry Kissinger

Henry Kissinger served as national security advisor and secretary of state under presidents Richard Nixon and Gerald Ford and also as a consultant to presidents John F. Kennedy, Lyndon Johnson, and Ronald Reagan. In the following viewpoint he warns that key events in 1999—such as the accidental bombing of the Chinese embassy in Belgrade by U.S. forces during the Kosovo conflict in May, as well as the release of the Cox report have contributed to rising tensions between the United States and China. Kissinger maintains that U.S. hostility toward China is unwarranted and rejects claims that China's military build-up and economic prosperity threaten the United States or democratic Taiwan. Kissinger calls on leaders in both nations to halt the rush toward confrontation.

As you read, consider the following questions:

1. What three propositions constitute the "case against China," in Kissinger's view?
2. In the author's opinion, how is China's strategic situation more problematic than the Soviet Union's was?

Reprinted from "Dangerous Drift," by Henry Kissinger, *Los Angeles Times*, September 12, 1999. Reprinted with permission from the author.

P resident Clinton meets with his Chinese counterpart, Jiang Zemin, at an international forum in New Zealand [in September 1999] amid the greatest strain in Sino-American relations since diplomatic contact was re-established in 1971.

Mounting Tensions Could Lead to Disaster

Many in Washington perceive Beijing's reaction to the American attack on the Chinese embassy in Belgrade as deliberate fostering of anti-American sentiments, and the Chinese military build-up and human rights practices as challenges to basic American interests and values. The view from Beijing is that the bombing of its Belgrade embassy was deliberate and that denial of World Trade Organization (WTO) membership, human rights accusations and charges of espionage are symptoms of America's unwillingness to allow China to play a role on the world stage.

In this atmosphere, Taiwan's sudden and unilateral challenge to the existing political understandings in the Taiwan Strait—at a time when a senior Beijing representative was preparing to visit Taipei for the first time—is interpreted in Beijing as the culmination of an American plot to divide China. [On July 9, 1999, Taiwan president Lee Teng-hui called for "special state-to-state relations" between China and Taiwan, challenging the Chinese government's position that Taiwan is part of the People's Republic of China.] Chinese warnings of a possible military response have taken on a severity reminiscent of the prelude to the Chinese intervention in the Korean War in 1950. In turn, many in Washington consider these Chinese expressions of concern as pretexts for executing long-held designs. Amid such mutual incomprehension, conflict, even military conflict, could suddenly erupt.

Three high-level visits—of Jiang Zemin to Washington [in November 1997], of Clinton to China [in June 1998] and of Prime Minister Zhu Rongji to Washington [in April 1999]—have accomplished little more than to assuage these trends. In each, atmospherics took precedence over substance, and in the Zhu visit American domestic politics blocked the conclusion of the WTO agreement that Zhu had been given reason to expect.

Some are fatalistic about this drift toward confrontation. Others compare the emergence of China to the rise of Germany before World War I, the implication being that, since a showdown is foreordained, better now, when China is still relatively weak. They forget that, in the eyes of history, the sin of the statesmen of that period was their failure to arrest the catastrophe that nearly destroyed European civilization.

A Sino-American conflict would be similarly avoidable and damaging to both sides. Both sides need a respite from the febrile mood of the moment. The atmosphere for this is not favorable in either country. Anti-American nationalism seems to be gaining momentum in Beijing. In America, a growing consensus in which China replaces the Soviet Union as our main enemy stultifies a necessary debate. Doubters of the dominant trend are accused of appeasement or of acting for their own economic benefit—a charge to which I have been subjected because I am chairman of an international consulting company. Anybody believing this charge should stop reading here.

No single component of American foreign policy can be an end in itself. We have security, political and economic interests and commitments in Asia that we will not sacrifice to our interest in constructive relations with China, however important we judge these to be. But the prospects of world peace, stability and progress will be jeopardized if the current unnecessary rush toward confrontation is not reversed by both sides.

The Case Against China

The case against China boils down to three propositions:

- That China, like the Soviet Union, is ideologically bent on regional, if not world, domination. Coexistence being impossible, we must maintain pressures on this last major totalitarian state until it transforms itself into a peaceful and cooperative democratic society.
- That China's military build-up coupled with the growth of its economy inevitably challenges the U.S. position in Asia and should be stifled before it takes on unmanageable proportions.
- That a military showdown over Taiwan is sufficiently

127

probable that we must take all measures in defense of Taiwan, even if these measures make such a conflict inevitable.

But is China really comparable to the Soviet threat to the United States?

Soviet ideology claimed universal applicability, and Soviet leaders as late at the '70s proclaimed the goal of the worldwide triumph of communism. Moscow avowed its determination to maintain communist parties in power, by force if necessary, intervening in Hungary and Czechoslovakia and threatening to do so in Poland and even in China.

The Chinese communist leadership makes no such claims; it exploits no international network of communist parties or radical forces to undermine Western positions. While many repressive aspects of a one-party state continue, there has been a vast improvement since [Communist leader] Mao and the Cultural Revolution [his attempt to transform Chinese society].

The debate over whether human rights should play a role in the conduct of our foreign policy has been won by the activists. But when the stakes are so high, these concerns need to be brought into some relationship with other objectives of American foreign policy. And the experiences of Haiti, Somalia and today in Kosovo should inspire some caution about how easy it is to impose our values.

Overstating China's Military and Economic Power

Even greater perspective is needed with respect to Chinese military power. The Soviet Union possessed some 2,500 strategic delivery vehicles, most with multiple warheads and many with high accuracy. An attack on the United States was technically feasible and strategically not inconceivable. The Chinese strategic force of some 25 liquid-fueled missiles with single warheads requiring hours to get ready is not an instrument for offensive operations. And when, in perhaps 10 years, the Chinese acquire multiple warheads for a larger number of missiles, an American missile defense—which I have always favored—should substantially preserve the strategic balance.

As for Chinese ground forces, they are at a level of the technology of the 1960s, capable of defending the home country but not suitable for offensive operations against a major opponent—including Taiwan. And around its periphery, China must cope with a strategic situation far more problematic than was the Soviet Union's in Europe. The Soviet Union threatened weak neighbors unable, either alone or in combination, to resist Soviet ground forces. But, from India to Japan to Russia, China faces militarily significant neighbors. If truth serum were administered to China's military leaders, they would probably be much more concerned with defending their frontiers than with expanding them militarily.

Neither a Superpower nor a Rogue State

Despite frequent alarms about the supposed China threat, China is not an emerging superpower. Although economically China has experienced rapid growth, militarily, China has been in relative decline since the 1970s. China does not and will not pose in the foreseeable future the kind of military threat to the U.S. that the Soviet Bloc did (exaggerated though that threat often was). China is not even an irritating "rogue state" as some consider Iraq, Iran, or North Korea. China has achieved normal commercial and diplomatic relations with the U.S. and most of China's neighbors. Even where there is tension, as in China's relations with Taiwan, India, and Vietnam, relations have improved considerably since the armed clashes of decades ago. Both the relative decline in China's military capabilities and the improvement of China's foreign relations should lead to U.S. optimism and confidence about the prospects for continued peaceful progress in Asia.

James H. Nolt, *In Focus: U.S.-China Security Relations*, April 8, 1999.

As for the Chinese economy, though China has grown at the average rate of 10 percent a year for much of the last 20 years, no country has ever maintained such a rate indefinitely. Nor is China doing so today. Its current growth of about 6 percent barely keeps pace with the growth of the Chinese labor force, leaving little room for a major increase in the percentage of the gross domestic product devoted to defense spending without risking the shipwreck of the Soviet Union.

To be sure, as China develops what it calls its "comprehensive national strength," its military power will grow. But, for the foreseeable future, the United States possesses diplomatic, economic and military advantages to enable us to shape the future confidently. Should China threaten the regional balance of power or our vital interests, we are bound to resist. But on proliferation, Asian economic progress and on stabilizing potential trouble spots such as South Asia and Korea, there are enough points of congruence to render a permanent geopolitical dialogue between China and the United States indispensable.

For us to imagine that we can prevent China's natural growth and emergence as a major power is to commit us to an unprecedentedly domineering role. Over time, this would drain our physical and psychological resources, be opposed by the rest of the world and, in the end, by the American people.

Controversy over Taiwan

Taiwan is the most explosive issue. Taiwan was part of China until 1895 when Japan annexed it, its first step toward conquest on the mainland. Starting with World War II, American presidents have affirmed Taiwan to be a part of China in one form or another: Franklin Roosevelt in 1943; Harry Truman in 1945; Richard Nixon in 1972; Jimmy Carter in 1979 and Ronald Reagan in 1982. The Reagan communique moreover stated that the United States had no intention of "pursuing a policy of two Chinas, or one China, one Taiwan"—a formula repeated 16 years later by Clinton in Shanghai. Since 1971, each president has firmly stated America's abiding concern for a peaceful resolution of the issue—a euphemism for opposition to the use of force—as did the Taiwan Relations Act of 1979, which adopted the principle as American law.

Within this framework, Taiwan has prospered, become democratic and increasingly participated in international forums that did not require formal state-to-state relations. At the same time, the United States, like the vast majority of the world's governments, was recognizing Beijing as the legitimate government of all of China. But, unlike most other countries, we were supplying the vast majority of the weapons for what was being treated officially as part of another country. For 30 years, China, while insisting on ultimate unification, nevertheless on several occasions expressed its willingness to defer a final resolution in the interest of its relationship with other countries, especially the United States. It did so provided Taiwan did not stake a formal claim to sovereignty. The United States, while repeatedly reaffirming its opposition to the use of force, did so invariably within the framework of a "one China" policy.

This complex framework should not be trifled with. Indeed, it is very much in Taiwan's own interest. For the key constraint on China's Taiwan policy has been China's stake in its relationship with the United States. Were Taiwan to achieve formal American recognition of a separate status, as its president now seems to seek, this would surely lead to some kind of military clash that, whatever its outcome, would permanently rupture Sino-American relations and isolate America in Asia and probably the world. Taiwan would be less, not more, secure in such an environment.

Thus, when President Clinton and Jiang Zemin meet, they must try to defuse the immediate crisis and begin to place Sino-American relations on a solid basis. Slogans like "strategic partnership" without content cannot substitute for a careful examination of where interests are congruent and where they need to be reassessed or managed.

With respect to Taiwan, three steps are needed: 1) to leave no ambiguity about America's opposition to the use of force; 2) to make clear that there is no change in America's longstanding acceptance of the principle of one China; (3) to insist on Taiwanese restraint in challenging a framework that, in fact, ensures their autonomy and without which events may well run out of control.

Cold War with China Must Be Avoided

A cold war would leave both sides in a classic no-win situation. China's economic progress would be stifled. Historically covetous neighbors might resurrect past ambitions. And, given the present disproportion of power, a military conflict would have grave consequences for China.

At the same time, Beijing would have many political cards to play. The Soviet Union, in the end, stood substantially isolated facing a coalition of all the industrial democracies plus China. But China has traversed its 5,000 years of recorded history by careful calculations of its necessities and great patience. No Asian nation will go along with a confrontational course unless provoked by Chinese pressures. Our European allies will distinguish their policies from ours and blame tensions on American high-handedness. Every crisis point, from Korea to the Middle East, would be exacerbated by a Sino-American cold—or hot—war.

Escape from this rush toward self-fulfilling prophecies requires a degree of bipartisanship not in great supply at this moment. Once the die is cast for confrontation, there will be no easy way back from the precipice. Which of the statesmen who so exuberantly went to war in 1914 would not have jumped at a chance to review their decision when they looked back at the damage done to the civilization of Europe and the long-term peace of the world?

"Whatever China's intentions, its capacity to harm U.S. interests is severely limited."

China Does Not Pose a Military Threat to the United States

Bates Gill and Michael O'Hanlon

In the following viewpoint, Bates Gill and Michael O'Hanlon contend that, despite some observers' concerns about a possible conflict between the two nations, there is no reason to think that China could challenge the United States militarily. The authors note that China has the world's largest army, in terms of raw troop numbers—but point out that the United States far surpasses China in terms of military technology and equipment. China is completely unequipped to mount an effective attack on the United States, they maintain, and it is very unlikely that China's army could invade and hold Taiwan. Gill and O'Hanlon are senior scholars in the Foreign Policy Studies Program at the Brookings Institution.

As you read, consider the following questions:

1. How many nuclear warheads does the United States possess, according to Gill and O'Hanlon, and how many does the People's Republic of China have?
2. What percent of China's military will have "late Cold War" weaponry by the year 2010, according to the Defense Intelligence Agency estimate quoted by the authors?
3. About how many ground troops does Taiwan have, according to Gill and O'Hanlon, and how many men is China capable of transporting to Taiwan at once?

Reprinted from "Power Plays: Why There's Less to the Chinese Threat than Meets the Eye," by Bates Gill and Michael O'Hanlon, *The Washington Post*, June 20, 1999. Reprinted with permission from the authors.

Revelations [in 1999] that China acquired detailed information about advanced U.S. nuclear weapons, missile guidance systems and other defense technology are causing concern that America will soon lose its decisive military advantage over the world's most populous country. Those worries are unfounded.

This is not to minimize the gravity of [the] allegations by the Cox committee, the select panel of House members investigating reports of systematic Chinese spying in the United States. The committee, headed by Representative Christopher Cox (R-Calif.), concluded that the secrets the Chinese obtained might allow them to manufacture small powerful warheads to fit on the mobile intercontinental ballistic missiles (ICBMs) they are developing. And those missiles, capable of reaching the United States, could be made more reliable with the help of classified information that may have been improperly provided by Hughes Space and Communications Co. and Loral Space & Communications.

China's ability to strike the United States with nuclear weapons is not new; this has been the case since the early 1980s. Efforts to make its nuclear force more modern, reliable and survivable against attack are normal for a nuclear power such as China, and there is no reason to suppose they demonstrate aggressive intent against the United States. Despite the leaks of defense secrets, the United States will retain more than a 10-to-1 advantage in strategic warheads over China for many years to come. At present, the United States possesses more than 10,000 nuclear warheads of all types, China fewer than 500.

How Good Is China's Military?

So before we give way to alarm in the wake of the Cox report, we ought to look at a fundamental question: How good is China's military? The short answer is, not very good, and not getting better very fast. Whatever China's intentions, its capacity to harm U.S. interests is severely limited.

Although Chinese defense spending has grown in real terms during the 1990s, it still only totals about $65 billion, according to the highest common estimate. This is less than a quarter of what the United States devotes to its military, though China's armed forces are much larger than America's.

The military investment gap becomes clearer when you look at what the two countries have spent on hardware. The Pentagon owns roughly a trillion dollars' worth of modern military equipment. China's comparable total is less than $100 billion (the American B-1 and B-2 bomber forces alone are worth around $50 billion). China has a large air force, but owns only a few dozen top-line fighters and no intercontinental bombers. By contrast, all 3,000 or so of the U.S. Air Force, Navy and Marines' fighters are of modern technological vintage.

Cut off from the dynamism of the rest of the country's economy, Chinese industries tied to defense are largely bloated and inefficient. Implicitly recognizing these shortcomings, China has reshuffled the organization of its defense industry several times in the past 15 years. According to a Defense Intelligence Agency estimate, only 10 percent of China's armed forces will even have "late Cold War equivalent" weaponry by 2010.

China has by far the world's largest military, with 2.8 million troops—twice the U.S. number. Yet raw size can be deceiving. China has 2 million troops in its ground forces, but the Pentagon estimates that only about 20 percent of them are even able to move about within their own country due to a shortage of trucks and other equipment.

What about the caliber of China's manpower? Again, a recent Pentagon report is revealing. It states that Chinese troops are generally patriotic, fit and good at basic infantry-fighting skills. But it goes on to say that nepotism in the armed forces is rampant, that China's most intelligent and energetic men rarely make a career of the military, and that training remains rudimentary.

China's "Asymmetric" Approach to Warfare

Some might respond to these shortcomings by noting that the United States has underestimated Asian armies before. China itself inflicted major setbacks on the United States during the Korean War and could, in theory, be a tough adversary there again. However, we are most unlikely to confront China on the Asian mainland. Today's potential disputes center on the seaways and islands off China's southern coasts. In addition, the armed forces of the United States and its major northeast Asian allies, Japan and South Korea, have improved much more than China's in the last half-century.

Others might argue that China does not need to compete with the U.S. military head-on—weapon for weapon—and could opt instead to challenge U.S. interests through indirect or "asymmetric" approaches. Employing advanced cruise missiles, sea mines, submarines, imaging satellites, antisatellite weapons and electronic warfare techniques, China could wage what its strategists call "local war under high-tech conditions" to target American vulnerabilities—attempting to sink U.S. ships near Chinese shores, or attacking advanced electronic systems on which U.S. forces depend.

There are kernels of validity here—after all, militaries always seek to exploit an adversary's weaknesses. But China will have a very tough time translating such aspirations into capabilities. That is especially true if the United States attends to its own defense by making key systems redundant, hardening them against radiation and taking other precautionary measures.

Concerns That China Will Invade Taiwan

Moreover, asymmetric warfare can only get you so far. Consider the one area where U.S. and Chinese forces are most likely to clash: in a Taiwan Strait crisis. Should it invade Taiwan to reclaim the island it considers a breakaway province, China's army would need to land enough troops to have a chance of defeating Taiwan's quarter-million-strong ground forces (plus some fraction of its 1.5 million army reservists). It surely would need hundreds of thousands of men for that purpose. But China cannot even move that many forces overland into Mongolia or Vietnam. Its combined amphibious and airlift forces can accommodate only 20,000 troops in all.

What if China tried to simply blockade Taiwan to bring down the island nation's economy and force its capitulation? China would have a better chance of success in this type of operation. But Chinese ships and planes trying to conduct a blockade near Taiwan's shores would remain vulnerable to Taiwanese aircraft. If the United States provided a modest amount of help—for example, a few aircraft carriers to control the air and seaways east of Taiwan (where China would have a hard time attacking them), as well as antisubmarine warfare assets—China could not sustain the blockade and would suffer large losses in the effort.

Not a Serious Strategic Threat

The new commander-in-chief of U.S. Pacific forces, Admiral Dennis Blair, has declared that China will not represent a serious strategic threat to the United States for at least twenty years. In almost every respect, China's armed forces lag behind the U.S. military by at least a couple of decades; in many areas they even compare poorly with the "hollow force" that the United States fielded in the immediate wake of the war in Vietnam. And on matters ranging from the professionalism of its officer corps and troop morale to training and logistics, China's military is in even worse shape than that.

Bates Gill and Michael O'Hanlon, *National Interest*, Summer 1999.

Or China could barrage Taiwan with ballistic missiles carrying conventional warheads, killing thousands. China forcefully raised that possibility in 1995 when it fired four M-9 missiles into the sea north of Taiwan to express displeasure over a visit to the United States by the president of Taiwan. China has recently quintupled its medium-range missile forces based near the Taiwan Straits. But its ballistic missiles will be hard-pressed to defeat Taiwan's military or sink nearby U.S. ships. Again, China could hurt Taiwan, but could not itself benefit decisively from doing so.

Nothing fundamental about these conclusions will change in the next decade or more. Even leaving aside the United States for a moment, Taiwan may actually get the better of the near-term military competition with China, especially as it gets serious about passive and active missile defenses. It has a more technologically advanced economy than China, and is more willing to purchase weapons from other countries when necessary.

We do not offer these conclusions as an apology for the spy scandals, which resulted from poor U.S. security procedures and a less-than-friendly Chinese attitude toward the United States. The leaks should never have happened, and many of the Cox report's recommendations to prevent future leaks are worthy of implementation. But the military significance of these illicit data transfers has been blown out of proportion, risking excessive and counterproductive policy responses.

There is no doubt that China is a rising power. But it remains a developing country, with per capita income levels only about one-tenth those of the West. It has enormous problems, from farming to banking. China will need at least two decades to become a serious strategic rival to the United States. Meantime, the United States and its major Asian allies need to maintain their composure. Hysteria over the Chinese challenge is the wrong approach, for it creates the potential for inevitable tensions between Beijing and Washington—over Taiwan, human rights and weapons proliferation—to develop into serious crises rather than be patiently handled and gradually resolved.

"[China] knows that the West is far ahead of it, but that as the West slows and China picks up its pace, the West can be caught."

China Could Pose a Military Threat to the United States

Mark Helprin

Mark Helprin is the author of *Winter's Tale* and *A Soldier of the Great War*, a contributing editor of the *Wall Street Journal*, and a senior fellow at the Claremont Institute for the Study of Statesmanship and Political Philosophy. In the following viewpoint, he maintains that China is on its way to becoming a military superpower. He notes that China is currently upgrading its nuclear capabilities, and that the Chinese economy is soaring. Helprin predicts that by about 2015 China will have the ability to pour its economic strength into revitalizing its conventional military. Once this happens, he warns, China will probably be able to dominate the Asian mainland and become a serious rival to the United States.

As you read, consider the following questions:

1. To what does Helprin attribute Israel's victory in the 1967 Six-Day war against Egypt, Jordan, and Syria?
2. What three reasons does the author offer to explain the fact that in 1998 China spent $37.5 billion on defense, rather than $100 billion or more?
3. In Helprin's view, if China were to invade Taiwan, how might this lead to conflict between Japan and China?

Excerpted from "East Wind," by Mark Helprin, *National Review*, March 20, 2000. Copyright © 2000 by Mark Helprin. Reprinted with permission from the author. This is an abridged version of a longer article.

China calls each new edition of its most potent intercontinental ballistic missile (ICBM) East Wind. This lovely and suggestive name begs an assessment of China's capabilities and intentions, because it appears to contradict what China tells us of itself and what is most reassuring for us to believe.

By geography, history, and tradition, China has been remarkably self-contained. It seems to have an artificial horizon that allows it to be content within its own sphere and to internalize its upheavals rather than export them. It rejects what it calls "power politics," and shuns alliances. Of the almost 2.5 million soldiers of the world's largest army, it has detailed only 32 for international peacekeeping duties, fewer than provided by Estonia. After going to war in Korea, India, and Vietnam, it simply withdrew, as if it found existence beyond its borders painful.

The historical pattern of Chinese stasis and Confucian self-restraint is repeatedly cited by China as evidence that its foreign policy is neither interventionist nor expansionary. But as China's thinly veiled nuclear threat against the United States shows—as do its wars or objectives in Korea, Vietnam, Tibet, Taiwan, the Senkaku Islands, the Spratlys and Paracels, India, Laos, Burma, Kashmir, on the Amur, and in various Third World clients—even if this is mainly true, it is not entirely true. And even if it is mainly true, China may yet depart from its traditional course. . . .

"Rich Country, Strong Arms"

Greeks, Romans, Muslims, Mongols, Russians, British, and numerous others have possessed what the Arabic historian Ibn Khaldun called 'asabiya, a sense of group solidarity, unity of purpose, and esprit de corps: in short, the momentum of destiny, when a whole people comes alight with success. China is reaching for this.

And ours is the perfect era for it to abandon its predilection for looking inward, in that science, technology, and trade—the international currencies of power—will inevitably pull from isolation even those countries that are most deeply entrenched. China has modeled itself, either consciously or by extraordinary and meaningful coincidence, on Japan, another isolated, inward-looking Asian country that, shocked and humiliated by the West, programmatically set out to appropriate the skills of those who had bested it, and succeeded.

British and American bombardment impelled the Japanese to tame their warlords, do away with feudalism, restore central power, and begin to study the ways of the West with a vengeance. China—not long ago just as feudal, divided, conquered, and backward—has done exactly this. After the restoration of the Meiji emperor in 1868, the Japanese sought national unity, industrialization, and military strength, recognizing that they would proceed in that order. Their slogan was *fukoku kyohei*, "rich country, strong arms." Predominantly agricultural Japan was able after only a third of a century to marshal warships, built in European yards, to defeat a second-class European power (Russia), and then after another third of a century to come close to defeating the world's leading naval power (this time with a battle fleet built in Japanese yards), because, to quote the cardinal sentence in G.B. Sansom's *The Western World and Japan*, "The greater part of her early industrial effort was put into production of goods of direct or indirect strategic importance." Japanese students, officials, and businessmen methodically collected information in the West or from Westerners in Japan, and, although the Japanese imitated every aspect of Western culture, their characteristically disciplined focus was on industry and the military.

Patience and Resolve

For China, the stress of occupation and war continued on during the catastrophic Great Leap Forward, the Sino-Soviet split, and the Cultural Revolution. Only in the Seventies did the sky clear enough for it to envision and begin military-industrial modernization, encouraged by its assessment that war was not imminent with either the Soviet Union or the United States, and that China would therefore be allowed a long strategic pause in which to prepare. In 1978, during the Third Plenum of the 11th Party Congress, Deng Xiaoping consolidated his authority and established what came to be known as the 16-Character Policy: "Combine the military products; let the civil support the military." Like the Meiji *fukoku kyohei*, this represents a profound understanding of the relation of military to economic power. . . .

As described by General Zhao Nanqi, former president of the Academy of Military Science, "The essence of the change was to make full use of the period of relative peace without major wars and to pay close attention to making plans for our modernization drive." A review of the relevant literature, cross-checked with reference to expressed and executed military, economic, and social policy, makes clear that China understands that wars are won by preparing the entire culture, reforming it if necessary. China understands that the source of its modernization and empowerment will initially be the West, from which it must take what it needs. It understands and anticipates a lag time of 50 to 75 years, or more, and it is patient. It knows that the West is far ahead of it, but that as the West slows and China picks up its pace, the West can be caught. It is approaching this with the purposeful concentration of the Meiji and the angry resolve of Germany between the wars. Its task is to win the next war, whenever that may be, and its determination is not to be dismissed.

A Nation Gears Up

These are China's aims, but what of its potential? With both political and analytical brilliance, Deng Xiaoping was able to redirect China's energies according to the single principle that its strategic power depends upon its per capita GNP [gross national product]. It may seem obvious that the wealthier a country is, the more it can devote to its military, but understanding the particulars of this proposition is necessary for making a decent guess about what China may be able to do and when. . . .

A very big country with a sudden and previously unexperienced margin of abundance would have many closed avenues opened to it. That Israel, with only a few million people, was able to prevail against enemies with, initially, many times its GNP, is attributable not least to the fact that Israel's per capita GNP quickly surpassed those of its competitors. Now it is 16 times Egypt's, or, in purchasing power parity (PPP), 4.5 times. (For countries with well developed domestic arms industries—China, Israel—PPP is more accurate than the absolute measure, because for these countries hard currency is not required for military acquisition.) In 1950, Egypt's GNP was 4.5 times Israel's. The subsequent reversal was due to Israel's rate of economic growth, which from Israel's founding to shortly before the Six Day War averaged 11 percent per annum, the highest in the world. Israel's spectacular victory over its combined opponents in June of 1967 was foreshadowed by this, but at the time only a few analysts fully understood the connection.

China's Military Spending

Although recently growth has slowed, for the past two decades China has had among the highest rates of economic growth and capital reinvestment in the world, which is all the more significant given China's size. In the twelve years from 1986 through 1998, China tripled its GNP and doubled its absolute per capita GNP. It doubled its PPP per capita GNP in just the six years prior to 1998. At first glance one might think that it has used this great increase in margin to advance defense outlays concomitantly, in that these have increased from $5.8 billion in 1986 to $37.5 billion in 1998. But it hasn't. Adjusting for population increase, China's 1998 GNP was more than its 1986 GNP by $400 billion, from which, in keeping with the exhortations of the 16-Character Policy, it might have been perfectly reasonable to extract a military bite not of $37.5 billion but of $100 billion or more. Why have military outlays increased by a factor of six rather than of 16? For three reasons. First, in the rush of getting to where it is, China has become somewhat less stable and finds it necessary to buy social peace with a larger civilian share of GNP than might otherwise have been desirable. Second, China's expressed time frame for catching the West is 50 to 75 years, and capital investment is a far more efficient use of resources than the immediate diversion of them. Third, China's military echelons and industries are in a period of reformation and development, able to make use only of what their current organization and methods of operation allow them to absorb.

The still tremendous increase in military spending has been devoted to both the replacement of outdated armaments and the more professional training of smaller forces.

In a "military market basket" of ICBM-or-equivalent delivery vehicles, major surface combatants, submarines, tanks, and combat aircraft, China has seen during its period of extraordinary growth a reduction of 22 percent (excluding the nuclear component, which has grown by 560 percent). If it holds military outlays to between 5 percent and 6 percent of GNP and the GNP continues its strong growth, the reductions will slowly stabilize and reverse. This is undoubtedly the scenario from which Western governments develop their estimates. But for China merely to continue along such a line would be a departure from the carefully formulated, widely propagated plan that it has been following for almost a generation. After the cadres have been professionalized and their weapons improved at a comfortable pace, and when the military industries have been adequately primed, China will find itself at a new juncture, probably sometime between 2015 and 2030.

If at that moment social stability need not be bought, or if the economy is strong enough for more butter and more guns, GNP will be diverted from civilian consumption and capital reinvestment to military expansion. Neither minor nor short lived, such a diversion will mean an immense surge in military spending and preparation, after which Western politicians will express their utter shock, and the press will declare enough times to convince itself absolutely that no reputable analyst could have foreseen or did foresee such a thing. Even then, it will not occur to the politicians or the press, as they pass helplessly from denial to hysteria, that during the previous years the Chinese mantra of stability so contemptuously derided in the West was not merely attributable to deep fear of the anarchy and dissolution that has so tried China during its long history, but was, rather, a grave effort to shield the 16-Character Policy in its early and vulnerable stages. This is undoubtedly for the Chinese leadership, as it moves through China's traditional perils, a matter of some drama and import, as it should be for us as well. . . .

What China Can Do

Even were China to realize its capacities, what could it do with its newfound power? Attendant to the flawed notion that China is bound by history to non-expansion is the impression that it has nowhere to go, being confined by the Himalayan, Karakorum, and Pamir mountains to the west; Siberia, leading north to nothing; Southeast Asia, an inverted triangle disappearing into the sea; and, to the east, the Pacific. Upon closer inspection, however, China's confines appear less than absolute.

"DON'T WORRY...EVERYTHING'S UNDER CONTROL..."

Gary Brookins for the *Richmond Times-Dispatch*. Reprinted with permission.

The Organization for Economic Cooperation and Development estimates that world petroleum use will double by 2030, with Middle Eastern supply of world demand peaking at approximately 55 percent between 2012 and 2020 (coincident with the Chinese surge that I project). Thus it is significant that, whereas the naval port of Zhanjiang is 4,800 miles from Abu Dhabi, Norfolk is 8,200 miles via Suez and, in view of Chinese relations with states along the Red Sea, 11,600 miles via the Cape of Good Hope. (The oil embargo that began in 1973 was successful not because of sudden Arab resolution but due to the effect of shuttling Persian Gulf tankers that great distance around the blocked Suez Canal.) Given the possibility that an advance upon contiguous Central Asian energy reserves might be for China not that much more daunting than its inhalation of Tibet, much opportunity exists here for what the Chinese call power politics, especially were China, like most developing nations, to shift from coal to oil.

Without using neutron bombs on swarms of short-range missiles, both of which it possesses and is augmenting, China has neither the amphibious capacity nor the air power to take Taiwan. But with a capitulationist, disengaged, or weakened United States, this would require only assiduous planning, moderate sacrifice, and medium economic growth. Beyond that, and possibly in the flush of unification, the domination of Japan cannot be ruled out as a future Chinese aim born not of ambition but of the cascade of events. A Chinese invasion of Taiwan would almost certainly stimulate Japanese rearmament, which would require of China the "active defense" that would (in the formulation of the Chinese Air Force) "teach a lesson and severely punish anyone who is threatening China's peace and security." China often proclaims peaceful intentions but simultaneously declares an extremely low threshold of preemption. Action against Japan before it has rearmed and while circumstances favor China, though perhaps unlikely, is the kind of unexpected tragedy that litters history.

China Will Be Able to Dominate Asia

With comparatively little effort, China can seal its obvious advantages in regard to a war on the Asian mainland. Its first steps are more or less accomplished, the consequence of its mass, its position, and the social transformation of the West. What American president in our time would go to full-scale non-nuclear war on the mainland of Asia, and what for? Truman, Eisenhower, and Johnson opted out when the U.S. possessed absolute nuclear superiority and different civilian and military cultures. Domination of the East Asian landmass is for China more or less assured.

Why then does it pour so much capital and energy into a full-blown nuclear-weapons program with the object of deploying MIRVed [multiple independently-targetable reentry vehicle] ICBMs on mobile launchers rolling around its great interior deserts, or in nuclear submarines cruising within protected maritime bastions? Clearly, its aim is to neutralize American nuclear superiority, or—as Maj. Gen. Yang Huan, formerly of the Strategic Rocket Forces, elegantly expresses it—to "smash nuclear blackmail." [General Douglas] MacArthur advocated and, later, Eisenhower considered the use of nuclear weapons against China, but nothing followed. Vietnam was a decade-long illustration of American nuclear restraint. China knows both that tactical nuclear weapons, having been all but banished from American doctrine, are not the easy route to escalation they once were, and that North Korean chemical and biological warfare programs make the tactical use of nuclear weapons on the Korean Peninsula unlikely. But China sees the urgency of neutralizing American nuclear power (which, with an invulnerable counterforce, it can). Why? To remove the nuclear dimension of localized warfare, freeing conventional means (in which China can more easily secure an on-scene advantage) to work without inhibition. As it becomes a great power, China envisions what has always been natural for a great power: the unchallenged dominance of its region of the world. Were China, as current American policy baselessly assumes, to lack such ambitions, it would be the first great power in history, including the United States, to do so.

Periodical Bibliography

The following articles have been selected to supplement the diverse views presented in this chapter. Addresses are provided for periodicals not indexed in the *Readers' Guide to Periodical Literature*, the *Alternative Press Index*, the *Social Sciences Index*, or the *Index to Legal Periodicals and Books*.

Elliott Abrams and Michael Ledeen	"American Power—for What?" *Commentary*, January 2000.
Bates Gill and Michael O'Hanlon	"China's Hollow Military," *National Interest*, Summer 1999. Available from P.O. Box 622, Shrub Oak, NY 10588-0622.
Michael Hirsh and Melinda Liu	"A Goose Step into the Future: China's 50th Anniversary," *Newsweek*, October 11, 1999.
David M. Lampton	"China," *Foreign Policy*, Spring 1998.
James Lilley and Carl Ford	"China's Military: A Second Look," *National Interest*, Fall 1999.
Richard Lowry	"Compromised: The Cox Report," *National Review*, June 14, 1999.
Johanna McGeary	"The Next Cold War?" *Time*, June 7, 1999.
Ross H. Munro	"Taiwan: What China Really Wants," *National Review*, October 11, 1999.
Jim Risen	"New Chinese Missiles Seen as Threat to U.S.," *New York Times*, September 10, 1999.
Stephen L. Schwartz	"China's Nukes: A Phantom Menace," *New Perspectives Quarterly*, Summer 1999.
Warren P. Strobel	"America's Stolen Thunder: The Cox Report," *U.S. News & World Report*, June 7, 1999.
Patrick E. Tyler	"Who's Afraid of China?" *New York Times Magazine*, August 1, 1999.
Caspar W. Weinberger	"Panama, the Canal, and China," *Forbes*, October 4, 1999.

CHAPTER 4

What Principles Should Guide U.S. Foreign Policy Toward China?

Chapter Preface

One of the most sensitive issues in U.S.-China relations is the status of Taiwan. Officially, the People's Republic of China (PRC) considers this island off the southeastern coast of the mainland part of its territory. However, Taiwan maintains its own government and enjoys extensive economic relations with the United States.

The origins of Taiwan's ambiguous status can be traced to the end of World War II, when a civil war between China's two dominant political parties came to a head. The nationalist Kuomintang party, led by Chiang Kai-shek, and the Communist Party of China, led by Mao Zedong, had fought each other since the 1920s. By 1949, the Kuomintang had been forced to flee to Taiwan. However, they still claimed to be the rightful rulers of China. Meanwhile, on October 1 of that year, Mao proclaimed the Communist revolution successful, and the People's Republic of China was born.

All this occurred at the dawn of the West's cold war with the Soviet Union. The United States, opposed to the spread of communism, initially refused to recognize the PRC, and instead made promises to support the exiled government on Taiwan. However, by the start of the 1970s, it was apparent that the PRC was firmly in power and that the leaders on Taiwan had little influence in mainland China. Over the objections of the United States, the United Nations admitted the PRC and revoked Taiwan's membership.

The United States now recognizes the Communist government in Beijing as the legitimate ruler of China. Yet U.S. leaders are reluctant to completely abandon ties with the government on Taiwan. Thus, ever since President Richard Nixon made the first official U.S. visit to the PRC in 1972, U.S. presidents have tried to maintain a delicate balance, helping to strengthen Taiwan economically and militarily without offending the PRC.

The status of Taiwan is just one of several divisive issues in U.S.-China relations. The authors in the following chapter debate the importance of Taiwan and other issues when considering the political and economic ties between the United States and the People's Republic of China.

*"The time has come for the United States to
. . . make clear that it will come to
Taiwan's defense if China uses force or even
threatens to use force."*

The United States Should Defend Taiwan Against China

William Kristol and Robert Kagan

In the following viewpoint, William Kristol and Robert Kagan, editors of the conservative magazine *The Weekly Standard*, argue that the United States should pledge to defend Taiwan in the event the People's Republic of China (PRC) attempts to invade or otherwise threaten Taiwan. Current U.S. policy on Taiwan is ambiguous, according to the authors: U.S. leaders have repeatedly implied that they would use force to defend Taiwan from Chinese aggression, but they have also discouraged Taiwan from openly declaring independence from mainland China. Kristol and Kagan believe this ambiguity could lead to war if Chinese leaders are not convinced of America's commitment to Taiwan. Writing a few months prior to the 2000 presidential primaries, Kristol and Kagan call on the Republican presidential candidates to make a clear promise to defend Taiwan.

As you read, consider the following questions:
1. In the authors' opinion, what "simple reality" should be the basis for American policy toward Taiwan?
2. What are the proposed provisions of the Taiwan Security Enhancement Act, according to Kristol and Kagan?

Reprinted from "Free Taiwan," by William Kristol and Robert Kagan, *The Weekly Standard*, July 26, 1999. Copyright © 1999 by News America Inc. Reprinted with permission from *The Weekly Standard*.

Taiwan's President Li Teng-hui sent the American foreign policy establishment into a nervous frenzy [in July 1999] when he declared that Taiwan would henceforth negotiate with China as one state to another. China experts are working overtime on their op-eds chastising Taiwan for its provocative action. And the Clinton administration has already made known its displeasure with Li's statements, denouncing them as unhelpful and reiterating the administration's own agreement with Beijing's one-China policy. Meanwhile, Beijing went nuclear, literally. In a document charmingly entitled "Facts Speak Louder Than Words and Lies Will Collapse on Themselves," Beijing informed the world of what the Cox committee and other investigations had already revealed: that it has a neutron bomb, just perfect for dropping on a nearby island that China would like to occupy. This threat will no doubt cause even more anxiety among American China hands, who will blame President Li for increasing the danger of another crisis in the Taiwan Straits.

Everyone should calm down. By carefully stripping away the absurd fictions of the "one-China" policy, President Li is actually doing all concerned a big favor. After all, it is true that "facts speak louder than words." The fact is that Taiwan is and has been a sovereign state for decades, with its own government, its own army, its own flag, its own flourishing economy, and full possession of its territory. Since the early 1990s, moreover, Taiwan has been a democracy, and nothing could be clearer than that the Taiwanese people want to remain separate from mainland China as long as that territory is ruled by a dictatorship. Until there can be one democratic China, they insist, there must be two Chinas.

Beyond the Shanghai Communique

These facts are, of course, inconvenient for the Clinton administration, which has adhered slavishly to the fiction of "one China" embodied in over a quarter-century's worth of Sino-American agreements. Beginning with the Shanghai Communique of 1972, the United States declared its understanding that both sides of the China-Taiwan dispute agreed that there was but one China. At the time of the Shanghai Communique, this was true in an odd sort of way. Both the

Communist government of Beijing and the authoritarian government of Chiang Kaishek's Kuomintang agreed that there was one China, and they both insisted it was theirs. The United States used this cute "one-China" formulation as a way of avoiding the issue. Anyway, the Cold War was on, and U.S. officials believed they needed China's help in containing the Soviet Union. If the price was a certain ambiguity and even some deception on the subject of Taiwan, so be it.

Twenty-seven years later, however, the world is a very different place. The people of Taiwan, now able to express their will electorally, have declared that they do not want to rule the mainland, and they do not want the mainland to rule them. There are two Chinas, not one. This puts an end to the smoke-and-mirrors game of the Shanghai Communique. The Clinton administration's spokesmen can say "one China" till they're blue in the face, but, to quote the Chinese government again, "lies will collapse on themselves." And then, of course, there is that other small difference between now and 1972: The Cold War is over. The Soviet Union is gone, and the biggest challenge to American interests in the world today comes from Beijing, not Moscow. With that rather large shift in global strategic realities, the need for ambiguity on Taiwan has disappeared.

The Dangers of Ambiguity

Indeed, ambiguity under the present circumstances has become dangerous. The fact is, now and in the years to come, the United States will have to answer one simple question on Taiwan. If the people of Taiwan want to be treated as a sovereign state and refuse to be reunited with the dictatorship on the mainland, as they do, and if China insists that Taiwan must be reunited with the mainland, by force if necessary, as it does, the question is this: Will the United States come to Taiwan's defense if and when these conflicting desires lead to military confrontation?

Until now, the United States has tried to avoid giving a clear answer to this question. The U.S. government has repeatedly expressed its opposition to any effort to settle the Taiwan matter by force. . . . But we have also left open the possibility that if war starts as a result of provocative statements by Taiwanese leaders, then we might just stand by and do nothing. That was the not-so-subtle warning delivered in person to the Taiwanese by former secretary of defense William Perry, visiting Taiwan at the behest of the president [in early 1998]. The name for this policy of studied equivocation has been "strategic ambiguity," and the logic behind it is that any promise by the United States to come to Taiwan's aid will only encourage the Taiwanese to declare independence.

An Easy Choice

The question presents itself these days, awkwardly and inescapably as always, in the matter of Taiwan and China. Whose side are we on?

On the one hand, we have Taiwan, which is an ally and a democracy. It is not a perfect ally nor a perfect democracy (but neither is the United States). Formed out of the nationalist movement that lost China to Mao's Communists, Taiwan increasingly has wished for independent statehood. In recent years, as the island has become more democratic and more wealthy, it has become more aggressive in expressing this wish.

On the other hand, we have China. The People's Republic is a doddering, desperate despotism, in which a corrupt oligarchy presides, only by the power of the gun, over a billion people who would rather live in freedom. China has always regarded Taiwan as an illegitimately errant province, ultimately to be subjugated to Beijing's rule. In recent years, as China's rulers have found themselves increasingly uneasy on their thrones, they have attempted, in the usual last refuge of dictators, to excite popular support by threatening belligerence against an exterior enemy—in this case, Taiwan.

Michael Kelly, *Washington Post*, July 28, 1999.

But if history is any guide, it is precisely this kind of ambiguity that leads to miscalculation and war. American words and American security commitments now need to conform to reality. And the reality is that if the people of Taiwan choose to remain a separate state, and if China responds with force or the threat of force, no American president would refuse to come to Taiwan's defense. Principle would demand that we act, and by the way, so would America's strategic interests. The incorporation of Taiwan by the present Chinese government—even if accomplished peacefully—would be a disaster for the United States and its East Asian allies. Imagine what our allies in the region would think about American staying power in the Pacific if we accepted such a crushing strategic setback without lifting a finger.

The United States Must Defend Taiwan

This simple reality should become the basis of American policy toward Taiwan. The Shanghai Communique is in fact no more relevant to our present strategic circumstances than that other great agreement of 1972—the ABM [antiballistic missile] treaty. The time has come for the United States to do away with a dangerous ambiguity and make clear that it will come to Taiwan's defense if China uses force or even threatens to use force.

Such a test may well come. . . . It would hardly be surprising if China were to respond to President Li's statement with another show of force. In 1996, it fired ballistic missiles into the sea near Taiwan's main harbors. This time, China may threaten a blockade of the entire island or take some other action to frighten the Taiwanese into backing off from their recent statements. If China does take such action, the United States should not hesitate to send the Seventh Fleet to Taiwan's waters, just as it did in 1996. In fact, the administration ought to send some ships there now, as a clear warning to the Chinese that they should not even consider any threatening military action. China hands will complain that this raises tensions. In fact, deterring the Chinese now is the best way to avoid a bigger crisis later. The less ambiguous U.S. actions are, the less chance there is that the Chinese will make a dangerous miscalculation.

There are also important steps Congress can take to clarify matters. Senate Foreign Relations Committee chairman Jesse Helms, joined by Democratic senator Robert Torricelli, has proposed important legislation—the Taiwan Security Enhancement Act—aimed at strengthening security ties between the United States and Taiwan and increasing Taiwan's own ability to deter hostile action by the Chinese. The Helms bill calls for lifting restrictions on arms sales to Taiwan, ending the ban on high-level military exchanges between the United States and Taiwan, and providing Taiwan with key weapons systems, including theater missile defenses, that would make it much harder for the Chinese military to use or even threaten force against Taiwan. Republicans—especially those who claim to be concerned about the increasing threat China poses to American interests—should take the lead in passing this legislation. [Editor's note: The House of Representatives passed the Taiwan Security Enhancement Act in February 2000; further action on the bill is not expected until after the 2000 presidential election.]

There is also a presidential campaign underway. The next president will inevitably be confronted by the Taiwan problem. His ability to deal effectively with any crisis will be affected by decisions taken now. Yet so far we have heard little from the leading Republican candidates about the brewing cross-straits crisis. Senator John McCain rightly stood up for the people of Kosovo under attack by the brutal dictatorship in Belgrade. Does he have a similar concern for the well-being of the democratic people of Taiwan? George W. Bush pointed out, correctly, that China is a strategic competitor of the United States, not a strategic partner, and he declared, also correctly, that American policy in Asia should first and foremost aim at protecting our friends and allies. Well, Taiwan is one of those friends. Do Bush and McCain and the other presidential candidates support the right of the Taiwanese people to determine their own future? Do they oppose the Clinton administration's outdated "one-China" policy? And do they support passage of the Taiwan Security Enhancement Act? These are important questions. Those who want to lead the United States and the world in the [twenty-first] century need to give some answers.

> "*Washington should reduce America's*
> *risk exposure by making it clear that*
> *the United States would not intervene in*
> *a [People's Republic of China]-Taiwanese*
> *struggle.*"

The United States Should Not Defend Taiwan Against China

Ted Galen Carpenter

Ted Galen Carpenter is vice president for defense and foreign policy at the Cato Institute, a conservative think tank in Washington, D.C. In the following viewpoint, he maintains that Americans do not want to go to war with China in order to defend Taiwan. Carpenter argues that such a conflict would be disastrous, especially considering that China is a nuclear power. On the other hand, he also believes that a successful Chinese attack on Taiwan would seriously damage U.S. interests in the Pacific region. Carpenter suggests that a better way for the United States to ensure Taiwan's security would be to sell better weapons to Taiwan, including submarines and antiballistic missiles. This would discourage China's willingness to initiate a conflict with Taiwan while also reducing the need for America to become militarily involved in the region.

As you read, consider the following questions:

1. In the author's opinion, how did Bill Clinton change U.S. policy on Taiwan when he visited China in June 1998?
2. What weapons systems does the author say the United States has already sold to Taiwan, and what systems does he believe should be made available to Taiwan in the future?

Excerpted from "Let Taiwan Defend Itself," by Ted Galen Carpenter, *Cato Policy Analysis*, August 24, 1998. Reprinted with permission from the Cato Institute.

An especially controversial aspect of President Clinton's June 1998 trip to China was his statement, following meetings with Chinese president Jiang Zemin, that "we don't support independence for Taiwan, or two Chinas, or one Taiwan, one China. And we don't believe that Taiwan should be a member in any organization for which statehood is a requirement." Administration officials subsequently insisted that U.S. policy had not changed, but those assurances were greeted with widespread disbelief in both the United States and Taiwan. That skepticism is understandable. Although Clinton stopped short of accepting Beijing's position that Taiwan is nothing more than a renegade province of the People's Republic of China (PRC), the opposition not only to Taiwanese independence but to Taiwan's hopes for lesser forms of international recognition confirmed a major change in Washington's position.

Previous U.S. policy was encapsulated in the deliberately ambiguous language of the 1972 Shanghai Communiqué at the end of President Richard Nixon's historic journey to China: "The United States acknowledges that all Chinese on either side of the Taiwan Strait maintain that there is but one China and that Taiwan is a part of China. The United States Government does not challenge that position. It reaffirms its interest in a peaceful settlement of the Taiwan question by the Chinese themselves."

Clinton's statement drew condemnation from the Senate GOP leadership and from sources as politically diverse as the *Wall Street Journal* and the *Washington Post*. The *Post* argued that the president had significantly reduced Taiwan's bargaining power in any cross-straits negotiations and questioned the propriety of the United States' ruling out "independence or any other option the Taiwanese people might choose." The *Journal* was more caustic, contending that Jiang "got his number one priority, Mr. Clinton carving the next slice of salami toward the Chinese goal of getting the U.S. to coerce Taiwan to join China, or alternatively, to stand aside while China invades." And Parris Chang, a member of Taiwan's Legislative Yuan and the head of the pro-independence Democratic Progressive Party's mission in the United States, bitterly accused Clinton of "selling out" Taiwan.

Although concern about the president's comments is justified, such criticisms misidentify the primary danger arising from Washington's policy shift. The *Journal's* interpretation is certainly overstated; Clinton explicitly reiterated those portions of the Shanghai Communiqué and other U.S. policy statements that emphasize America's insistence that the Taiwan issue be settled peacefully. There is little evidence that Washington will pressure Taiwan to accept Beijing's rule, and the Taiwanese would ferociously resist such pressure in any case. Nor is it likely that the United States would remain aloof if the PRC attacked Taiwan.

The real problem is that Clinton's policy has a built-in, extremely dangerous contradiction. His statements in Shanghai indicate that the United States now considers Taiwanese independence an illegitimate option. That is a far cry from merely acknowledging that most Taiwanese and mainland Chinese endorse the theoretical goal of "one China." The implications of that change in language go far beyond the escalation of U.S. opposition to Taipei's bid to join the United Nations and other international bodies.

More tangibly, Clinton's policy shift presages a reduction and eventual elimination of arms sales to Taiwan—as already suggested by several East Asia experts. Indeed, there are persistent news reports in the East Asian press that Chinese leaders received "private pledges" by "senior U.S. officials" to cut or downgrade arms exports to Taiwan. That is not a trivial matter, for a cutoff of arms sales could leave Taiwan highly vulnerable to PRC intimidation or outright military coercion within a decade.

The administration is not willing to follow its policy of accommodating Beijing to its logical conclusion, however, for that would require the United States to stand aside if the PRC did use military force. Instead, the president implies that the United States would not tolerate such action and would respond much as it did in early 1996 when China conducted provocative ballistic missile tests in the Taiwan Strait. At that time, Washington dispatched two aircraft carrier battle groups to the area and privately warned Beijing against any escalation. There is evidence that the PRC and the United States may have come much closer to armed conflict than Congress or the American people realized at the time.

In short, the administration has embarked on a course that combines the worst, most dangerous features of the competing policies of firmness and accommodation. Washington is committing itself to help isolate Taiwan politically and diplomatically and will come under mounting PRC pressure to help neuter the island militarily. Yet, if Beijing follows up on that advantageous situation and actually seeks to coerce Taiwan, the United States has indicated that it may (and probably will) shield Taiwan with American air and naval forces—at the risk of a disastrous U.S.-Chinese war.

Washington needs to adopt a course that is precisely the opposite of the one it is currently pursuing. The president should have informed Chinese leaders that it is not America's place to tell Taiwan whether or not to opt for independence. The United States should also refrain from making any commitment, either explicit or implicit, to prohibit arms sales to Taiwan and should "clarify" (renounce) any previous statements that imply otherwise. At the same time, U.S. officials need to make it clear to both Beijing and Taipei that under no circumstances will the United States intervene in a PRC-Taiwanese war. . . .

Competing Bankrupt U.S. Policy Options

Thus far, the debate about a new policy on the Taiwan issue has been dominated by two factions. Members of the first group believe that it is crucial for long-term U.S. interests in East Asia that Washington go to considerable lengths to accommodate Beijing's wishes. Such "accommodationists" are the most outspoken advocates not only of "engaging" China but of developing an extensive U.S.-PRC "strategic partnership." Although they shrink from openly consigning Taiwan to the PRC's tender mercies, the policies they advocate point ultimately to that outcome. The accommodationist view is now clearly making inroads at the highest levels of the Clinton administration.

The rival faction, centered in the conservative wing of the Republican Party, wants the United States to intensify, not reduce, its support for Taiwan. Members of that group express great admiration for Taipei's economic success, democratic reforms, and long-standing anti-communist credentials, and they increasingly accuse the administration of appeasing Beijing. The pro-Taiwan faction generally favors an explicit U.S. guarantee to defend the island if the PRC resorts to force, and some members openly urge Taiwan to declare independence and seek U.S. diplomatic recognition.

The course suggested by either faction could cause major problems for the United States. . . .

The Third Way: Enabling Taiwan to Defend Itself

Instead of trying to defend Taiwan, whether as part of a consistently pro-Taiwan policy or as a fall-back measure if the attempt to accommodate Beijing fails, Washington should reduce America's risk exposure by making it clear that the United States would not intervene in a PRC-Taiwanese struggle. The only politically feasible way of doing that, however, would be for Washington to liberalize its arms export policy and allow Taiwan to buy the weapons it needs to become and remain militarily self-sufficient. . . .

A promise to risk the lives of millions of Americans to defend Taiwan is a promise that rational Americans should never want their government to fulfill. The American people understandably admire the economic and political progress that Taiwan has made, and they have no wish to see the island forcibly absorbed into a still highly authoritarian PRC. Taiwan is also of some economic importance to the United States, since it is America's eighth largest trading partner. Nevertheless, Taiwan's political autonomy (or independence) falls far short of being the kind of vital interest for which the United States must be prepared to wage a major war. Even some hawks concede that, intrinsically, Taiwan is not a vital interest, but they contend that failure to defend the island against a PRC attack would destroy Washington's credibility throughout East Asia. Ross Munro, director of Asian studies at the Center for Security Studies, among others, argues that "if China succeeds in taking military control of Taiwan it would gain control of Asia's vital sea lanes and the entire balance of power in Asia would shift overwhelmingly in China's favor."

Munro's thesis exaggerates the extent of the sea-lane control Beijing would gain, but even if true, that is an argument for Japan, South Korea, Australia, and other East Asian powers to protect Taiwan. After all, the sea-lanes are in their region, not ours. If a hostile power threatened the sea-lanes in the Gulf of Mexico, no one would expect Tokyo, Seoul, and Canberra to defend them while the United States remained on the sidelines. There is simply no adequate strategic reason for the United States to risk war to defend Taiwan.

Breen. Reprinted with permission from Copley News Service.

A better option is to let Taiwan buy the weapons it needs for its own defense. It should be noted that Taiwan is not asking the United States to give the weapons as a form of foreign aid; Taipei is willing to pay top dollar for the various systems. Washington has been responsive to some requests; earlier this decade it approved sales of F-16 fighters, helicopters, and Stinger anti-aircraft missiles, for example. More recently, the Clinton administration agreed to sell several Knox-class Navy frigates along with rapid-fire Phalanx anti-aircraft guns and Harpoon anti-ship missiles—a deal valued at $300 million. However, U.S. officials have thus far declined to approve sales of other crucial items, including the sophisticated AIM-120 Advanced Medium Range Air-to-Air Missile and advanced versions of the air-to-surface Maverick missile. Given the Clinton administration's increasingly evident policy tilt toward Beijing, it is now even less likely that Washington will authorize such exports.

Prospects have also dimmed for two other [Taiwanese] objectives. The Taiwanese also want to buy attack submarines and develop, with U.S. assistance, an anti-ballistic-missile system, but Washington has thus far rebuffed both requests. Submarines are especially important to Taiwanese military planners because, unless [Taiwan] has at least a modest fleet of subs, Beijing's navy could someday dominate the Taiwan Strait.

A more responsive U.S. policy on such arms purchase requests from Taiwan would maximize the chances that Beijing would use only peaceful measures in its campaign to achieve reunification. Conversely, a militarily inferior Taiwan might tempt PRC leaders to consider using force and thereby precipitate an East Asian crisis. University of Pennsylvania political scientist Avery Goldstein emphasizes the importance of a military balance of power across the Taiwan Strait: "The point is not that Taiwan would easily be able to defeat an increasingly modern PLA [People's Liberation Army] assault. The point instead is that Taiwan's sustained military modernization will make it very costly for the PLA to prevail, even if others (most important the United States) choose not to intervene." That is the essence of a "porcupine" strategy—raising the probable costs to a would-be conqueror so high that no rational policymaker would contemplate launching a military strike.

That is Taiwan's best hope for eluding conquest or intimidation and America's best hope for escaping the nightmare of being called on to defend Taiwan against a PRC attack. A strategy based on Washington's willingness to help Taiwan become militarily self-sufficient offers the only realistic prospect of avoiding the Scylla looming as a result of the Clinton administration's policy of ambivalent appeasement or the Charybdis created by American warhawks who want to give an explicit pledge to shield Taiwan with U.S. military forces.

163

> *"The U.S. should curtail its commercial intercourse with China until Beijing has a government that will not use its gains for aggression."*

The United States Should End Free Trade with China

William R. Hawkins

Since the late 1980s, China has been seeking admission into the World Trade Organization (WTO). China's entry into the WTO would mean that the United States would be obligated to engage in free trade with China and grant it permanent Normal Trade Relations status. In the following viewpoint, William R. Hawkins maintains that China should not be admitted to the WTO. The U.S. trade deficit with China, he maintains, shows that the Chinese benefit from free trade with the United States much more than Americans do. Moreover, he warns that China is using the wealth generated from free trade with the United Sates to upgrade its military, thus threatening U.S. interests in the Pacific region. William R. Hawkins is a visiting fellow at the U.S. Business and Industry Council.

As you read, consider the following questions:

1. What was the U.S. trade deficit with China in 1998, according to the author?
2. In the author's opinion, what is the primary benefit that U.S. corporations will reap from trade with and investment in China, and what is the primary benefit that the Chinese government will receive?

Reprinted from "Don't Ask 'How,' but 'Why' Should China Be in the WTO," by William R. Hawkins, *IntellectualCapital.com*, November 4, 1999. Reprinted with permission from the author.

The Clinton administration is reportedly split over how to coax China into the World Trade Organization (WTO). Secretary of State Madeleine Albright and National Security Adviser Samuel Berger favor additional concessions to further demonstrate American goodwill. But U.S. Trade Representative (USTR) Charlene Barshefsky and National Economic Council Chairman Gene Sperling argue that given Beijing's unwillingness to negotiate, the U.S. should refrain from any major concessions, lest America end up negotiating against itself.

Both sides of this internal debate on China policy are wrong. It is not in America's national interest to bring China into the WTO, on any basis, as long as it is ruled by the present Communist regime.

Open Markets?

The commercial wing of the administration—represented by Barshefsky—thinks bringing China into the WTO will open a "big emerging market" for American exports. They touted a list of concessions allegedly made by Chinese Premier Zhu Rongji at the April [1999] summit with President Clinton, which would create new opportunities for American farmers, bankers and industrialists. This is an exaggeration. An assessment of the April terms requested by the USTR from the International Trade Commission (ITC) concluded that "the impact on the United States of the various tariff cuts considered is positive, but minor." The ITC finds this meager result "is consistent with the fact that U.S. trade with China accounts for less than 1% of U.S. GDP (Gross Domestic Product)." And by a margin of 5–1, that trade consists of exports from China, not from the United States.

The ITC also concluded, amazingly, that the U.S. trade deficit with China would actually increase if China joined the WTO. (The U.S. deficit with China has been exploding, hitting $57.4 billion [in 1998].) The ITC demolishes the notion that a WTO deal will throw open China's market. Beijing's WTO membership would make China a more secure place for foreign investors to build factories that would export to the U.S.

The actual results of China's entry would be even less beneficial than the ITC's assessment based on the administration's false hopes. Beijing denies it made the concessions the USTR claims it did, and on which the ITC report was based. Vice Premier Qian Qichen has called the U.S. demand for concessions a form of "economic aggression" similar to the 21 Demands imposed upon China by Japan in 1915. He called this the kind of "hegemonism" that leads to war.

Qian specifically objected to the opening of China's market to American farmers, bankers and industrialists. Beijing has insisted that if it comes into the WTO, it will be as a "developing country." As such, it is not interested in imported products, only in building its own industrial base and self-sustaining economy. This includes agriculture where Vice Finance Minister Zhang Youcai has announced plans to develop new wheat growing areas to reduce dependence on imports. Wheat is currently America's largest farm export to China.

Competing Visions

American corporations, which have been pushing hard for a China WTO deal, know they are not opening an export market. What business sees in China is a chance to profit from the development of Chinese capabilities. USA*Engage, a lobbying group representing over 500 firms, drools over China's 10-year plan for $750 billion in domestic infrastructure projects. General Motors has invested $2 billion in a new Buick factory in China while Microsoft is building a new research center there. A study by the U.S. Commerce Department's Bureau of Export Administration found that "the underlying and stated objectives of China's foreign investment and trade policies . . . are modernization and self-sufficiency of China's industrial and military sectors."

Beijing's economic policy conforms with the doctrine of Jean Baptiste Colbert, the finance minister for France's Louis XIV, who believed "trade is the basis of finance and finance is the sinew of war." The eminent historian of how economics affects the global balance of power, Paul Kennedy, has noted that "the more China pushes forward with its economic expansion in a Colbertian, *etatiste* fashion, the more likely that development will have power-political implications." It is

Feeding a Totalitarian Regime

China is not only a trade problem, it is a national-security problem. China is using the hard currency from its U.S. trade surpluses and international bank loans to buy submarines, destroyers, antiship missiles, and fighter aircraft from Russia and to build long-range missiles to reach the west coast of the United States. Yet, America permits China to launch U.S. satellites on Long March rockets, thus subsidizing the development of the Chinese strategic missile force.

America is taking a terrible risk feeding a regime, the character of which may be seen in its treatment of dissidents, Tibetans, Christians, and women pregnant with any child conceived in violation of China's barbaric one-couple, one-child policy. While America should seek no confrontation with China, we should treat Beijing as the great power it has become.

We cannot practice true free trade with a nation that has no independent judiciary, where labor is conscripted, corruption is endemic, U.S. goods face a 17 percent value added tax and a 23 percent tariff, and many of whose corporations are government fronts. The United States should cancel China's most-favored-nation status and negotiate a reciprocal trade agreement that recognizes our different societies and conflicting interests.

Patrick J. Buchanan, *The Great Betrayal: How American Sovereignty and Social Justice Are Being Sacrificed to the Gods of the Global Economy.* Boston: Little, Brown, 1998.

---

these implications that should be the concern of U.S. national policy-makers.

Unfortunately, Albright and Berger hold to the contrary utopian notion that commercial relations build an interdependence that promotes peace, and that increased wealth will tame China. The terms of trade are not as important as weaving this commercial web; thus they favor concessions to Beijing to make the WTO deal happen.

The Build-Up

China gave another example of how they will use their increased wealth when it recently announced the purchase of the first batch of Su-30 strike fighters from Russia. The $2-billion contract for 38 warplanes includes spare parts, tech support and weapons systems. The Su-30 has greater combat range than existing Chinese fighters and is expected to be used primarily in an antiship role. Beijing's modernization program—which also includes warships, submarines, airborne troops, and both cruise and ballistic missiles—is designed to project power into the Pacific, in the direction of American interests and allies.

It is the large, and growing, U.S. trade deficit with China that provides Beijing with the hard currency needed to buy advanced weapons. Investment in China, however, transfers enormous amounts of "dual use" technology critical to the creation of China's own military capabilities. The Bureau of Export Administration reports that "China's investment policies are geared toward shifting foreign investment into the central and western parts of China. . . . China's national laboratories and the majority of China's military/industrial enterprises are located in this region." Bringing China into the WTO will increase these financial and industrial resource flows, shifting the balance of power of the region.

The commercial axiom is that both parties benefit from trade and investment. In the case of commerce between American corporations and the Beijing regime, the gains to the corporations are in the form of private profits while the gains to the regime are in the growth of its military-industrial capabilities. This increase in China's strength poses threats to the stability of Asia. The public cost of meeting these threats swamp in scale and duration the private commercial gains. The U.S. should curtail its commercial intercourse with China until Beijing has a government that will not use its gains for aggression.

"We trade with China because exports create American jobs and improve Americans' standard of living."

The United States Should Not End Free Trade with China

Jerry J. Jasinowski

In the following viewpoint, Jerry J. Jasinowski argues that free trade with China benefits the United States. Free access to the 1.2 billion potential consumers in China helps U.S. businesses compete internationally, he maintains. In addition, U.S. economic engagement with China exposes the Chinese to American values such as free competition. If the Chinese embrace the value of freedom in trade and business competition, then freedom in other areas, such as politics and religion, will more easily follow. Jasinowski is president of the National Association of Manufacturers.

As you read, consider the following questions:

1. How many dollars' worth of commercial goods does the United States sell to China annually, according to Jasinowski?
2. In the author's opinion, why is China's admittance to the WTO in the U.S. national interest?
3. In Jasinowski's view, what reforms should be made to curb the sale of military technologies to China?

China's theft of U.S. nuclear secrets, combined with its disturbing record on human rights, makes many Americans question the basis of the U.S.-Chinese trade relationship. While this response is understandable, to curtail or even end trade with China would run counter not only to our national interests but could well foster the very behaviors of the Chinese government we find so troubling.

Let me be clear: The business community takes violations of our national security and abuses of human rights seriously. I served as an intelligence officer in Asia during the Vietnam War and later taught at the Air Force Academy. I respect the convictions of those who say we ought to terminate our economic relationship with China until the Chinese government reforms itself. But indignation is no substitute for careful thinking, and frustration must not replace a cool and thoughtful evaluation of where our national interests lie.

Congress already has imposed restrictions on the kinds of goods we can export—restrictions that often are arbitrary, excessive and ineffective. Consider this irony: The software technologies that protect our e-mail communications are available in every electronics store in the country. But in denying this type of software to the Chinese, we prevent Chinese citizens from enjoying the same protections Americans have and make them vulnerable to a government that consistently takes action against individuals seeking personal freedom.

So where should U.S.-Chinese relations go from here? What should be our priorities, and how should we advance them?

Asian Economic Growth Benefits the United States

First, economic growth in China is of paramount importance to Asian regional security and world stability and therefore must be a top U.S. priority. Some are urging Congress not to approve the president's decision to grant "most-favored-nation" status, which has come to be known as normal-trade-relations status, or NTR, for China. Yet this would damage our influence with the Chinese government while having little or no impact on the Chinese economy. The Chinese simply would buy the goods they now purchase from us elsewhere—namely, from our international-trade competitors who are eager to gain access to the Chinese marketplace.

In other words, we would lose if we curb our trade relationship with China. Trade with China is not a favor we do for Beijing. We trade with China because exports create American jobs and improve Americans' standard of living.

Currently, we sell about $14 billion worth of commercial goods to the Chinese annually, only a relatively small percentage of which has any potential national-security implications. [Since 1992], China has moved from being our 10th- to our fourth-largest trading partner. In nominal terms, U.S. exports to China have increased 252 percent since 1986. This contrasts with the overall growth of U.S. exports (200 percent) during the same period. Put in human terms, China has 1.2 billion people and urban infrastructures in need of significant improvement. These realities offer U.S. firms an opportunity to play active roles in constructing roads, bridges and buildings; creating and serving communications networks; and meeting the needs of a growing consumer class. We only have begun to scratch the surface of economic opportunity in the world's most populous country.

And for those who argue that trade costs Americans their jobs and higher incomes, consider: Plants that export their products grow jobs 18 percent faster than those that don't sell goods abroad. They pay, on average, 15 percent more, provide benefits that are 40 percent higher and are 10 percent less likely to go out of business. Even by the most conservative measures, exporter productivity is 20 percent better; some estimate that number to be 40 percent.

As to the large amount of commercial products we buy from China, for the most part these do not involve production jobs that have moved from places such as Kalamazoo, Michigan, to Shanghai. Rather, they reflect a shift in market share between Southeast Asia and China. During the last decade, as our trade deficit with China has increased, our trade deficit with the rest of Asia (not including Japan) has decreased. Furthermore, imports improve our standard of living, affecting the quality, price and variety of products American consumers are able to purchase. Quality, affordable imports are one of several factors that have spurred the astonishing success of our economy during the last decade.

Bringing Freedom to China

In addition, engagement with China enables us to demonstrate the value of freedom in very tangible ways. The competitive free market is premised on the idea that men and women are responsible enough to make good decisions about their economic lives. In the United States, we believe this principle applies to all facets of life—political, religious, family, etc. As we continue to interact with the Chinese at an economic level, does it not make sense that Chinese citizens will wonder why they, too, cannot have the same freedoms in their personal lives as in their economic ones?

It's worth noting that some of those most subject to repression support continued U.S. trade relations with China. It would be a great irony if a cut-off of U.S.-China trade actually precipitated greater tensions between the two countries and fostered the very actions on the part of the Chinese government many observers rightly find unacceptable.

Edwin J. Feulner Jr., president of the conservative Heritage Foundation, makes this point in his introduction to Heritage's book, *Strategies for U.S. Relations With China* (1997). "U.S. commerce and the attendant presence of U.S. companies in China play a significant role in expanding the frontiers of freedom for countless thousands of Chinese," he writes. "By drawing them into the private sector and away from the state-controlled economy, U.S. companies have lessened the degree of state intrusion into the day-to-day lives of their employees. We likewise believe the growing numbers of U.S. nongovernment organizations in China serve to attenuate state intrusiveness and to expand areas of freedom."

China and the World Trade Organization

There are three aspects of our trade relationship with China that deserve closer scrutiny. First, NTR with China offers the Chinese no special breaks. It merely allows the United States and China to trade without high tariffs and other barriers, thereby enabling citizens of both countries to benefit from one anothers' goods.

Second, allowing China to join the World Trade Organization, or WTO, would not be a favor we do the Chinese. To the contrary, it is a favor we would be doing ourselves.

China's fledgling market economy would have to continue undergoing substantial change in order to meet WTO membership criteria without the incentive of U.S. trade. It is in the U.S. national interest to have China inside the multilateral rules-based system provided by the WTO. Tying China to an international regime of trade laws would hold China accountable for its trade practices. A full reciprocal WTO relationship between the U.S. and China would provide China with permanent NTR status, thereby ending the annual fight about conventional trade with China. This, in turn, would ensure greater economic continuity in our relationship with the Chinese and focus on other dimensions of our political relationship with them.

Promoting Economic Stability in Asia

We must grant China permanent normal trade relations status. It's important to understand what that means: it simply means that we will give China the same tariff schedule we apply to most every other nation in the world, and China will do likewise. It would eliminate the annual vote on China's trade status, which we do not apply to any other WTO member. . . .

The economic benefits of this deal to America are clear. . . .

But I believe the economic benefits are only the beginning of the argument. For I am convinced that this agreement is as vital to our national security as it is to our economic security. . . .

As the President said when Premier Zhu Rongji visited Washington [in 1999], "if we've learned anything in the last few years from Japan's long recession and Russia's current economic troubles, it is that the weaknesses of great nations can pose as big a challenge to America as their strengths." So as we focus on the potential challenges that a strong China could present to the United States in the future, let us not forget the risks that could be posed by a weak China, beset by internal conflicts, social dislocation, criminal activity, and large-scale illegal emigration—a vast zone of instability in Asia.

Samuel R. Berger, remarks before the Woodrow Wilson International Center for Scholars, February 2, 2000.

The round of U.S.-Chinese WTO negotiations concluded earlier this year reportedly included substantial reductions in Chinese tariffs on U.S. industrial exports to China and full trading and distribution rights in China for U.S. companies.

China has agreed to liberalize the investment rules it historically has imposed on U.S. companies doing business in China, and also has committed to privatizing its state trading enterprises and to open and liberalize its service sectors, from insurance to professional services to foreign-service providers. The dispute-settlement mechanism in the WTO accord also would provide a credible and effective means of enforcing U.S.-Chinese tariff rates backed up by the threat of WTO-authorized sanctions for Chinese noncompliance.

What does all this mean for the United States? The most conservative estimates see the immediate impact of China's WTO accession as an increase in U.S. exports of goods and services to China of slightly more than $3 billion annually. Other estimates suggest that during the next few years this figure could grow to $13 billion. While accurate estimates are notoriously difficult to make, they nonetheless underline the fact that China, by joining the WTO, formally would commit to dramatic reductions in its tariff and nontariff barriers to U.S.- and other foreign-made products.

Export Controls on Military Technologies

Third, we need to bring substantial change to our erratic system of export controls. We need to evaluate exactly which technologies are related to our national security and which are not. And we need to make sure that, instead of the futile go-it-alone approach to export-control policy that too often has characterized U.S. policy in this area, we follow the recommendation of the Cox-committee report and work to develop a multinational export-control regime. This effort will, however, require leadership on the part of our government and will involve all the tools of diplomacy—compromise, persuasion and even the occasional threat. In a profound way, the unilateralism of current U.S. export-control policy represents the easy way out. It doesn't require the tough work that goes into actually leading our allies into a coalition on this issue. But it is this tough work that will help us craft multilateral agreements on export controls that will enable us truly to monitor who is selling what to the Chinese and to prevent the sale of technologies that could be used for military purposes.

Effectively ending trade with China in the name of national righteousness is emotionally appealing. But it would do no good and could do active harm. We need not consider China a friend, but nor must it become an enemy. China has become a major trading partner for the United States, one in which we can work to influence policy by virtue of example and, when appropriate, through diplomacy.

In the U.S. National Interest

Open trade between China and the rest of the world can abet political reforms. For those who care about the advancement of human freedom, such reforms are devoutly to be wished.

Trade with China is in the U.S. national and economic interest. It advances our agenda throughout Asia and helps maintain regional security. It provides us with a level of influence with the Chinese government we otherwise would not have. It enables us to advance our values among ordinary Chinese citizens who, many for the first time, are exposed to the freedoms we often take for granted. And if national interest is the goal of U.S. trade policy, trade with China sounds pretty American to me.

"[If China refuses to reform,] the US should use its unmatched military and economic power . . . to oppose, isolate, and undermine the current government of China."

The United States Should Pressure China to Adopt Democratic Reforms

Robert W. Tracinski

In the following viewpoint, Robert W. Tracinski, editor of the *Intellectual Activist*, criticizes U.S. foreign policy toward China under President Bill Clinton. Tracinski claims that Clinton's policy has been based entirely on appeasing China by giving it trade benefits and reducing criticism of China's human rights abuses. This strategy, writes Tracinski, is based on the idea that by engaging China economically and politically, the United States will gain more influence with Chinese leaders. However, Tracinski believes this approach is ineffective and inexcusable given the authoritarian nature of the Chinese government and its overt hostility toward the United States.

As you read, consider the following questions:
1. What examples does the author offer as evidence of China's brutality?
2. According to Tracinski, what is the "one unchanging rule" of the Clinton administration's China policy?
3. In the author's view, current U.S. policy toward China can be traced back to what president?

Excerpted from "America's Foreign Policy Surrender to China," by Robert W. Tracinski, *Intellectual Activist*, July 1998. Reprinted with permission from *Intellectual Activist*.

I magine that you live in an inner-city neighborhood threatened by a vicious Mafia gang. This gang has already taken over control of several previously legitimate businesses and is threatening to take over still others. In the process, it has murdered opponents and uses the threat of violent retaliation to keep the entire neighborhood in fear. You contact the police and they assure you that they are doing their best. They have decided to "engage" the Mafia leaders in a "dialogue." Their strategy, the chief of police explains, is to form a "partnership," dealing with the two sides' "differences" on a case-by-case basis. The police, he boasts, have already made progress; they have offered a number of concessions to the gang and received, in return, promises by its leaders to commit fewer crimes. When you suggest that the police should bring the full weight of the law down upon the gang's heads, you are scolded that such tactics would "isolate" and antagonize the gang. Above all, the chief emphasizes, the most important thing is for the police not to endanger good relations with the gang, lest they lose their "leverage" over it.

This, of course, would be a disastrous strategy; it would constitute a total surrender of the police to the criminals. Yet the Clinton administration is pursuing exactly this approach in dealing with the gang of dictators who rule China.

Chinese Brutality

The Chinese rulers' standard method for dealing with all enemies, foreign or domestic, is brutality. Consider only China's recent record (not counting the routine mass murders under Mao Tse Tung and the "Cultural Revolution"). China's foreign policy includes the continuing occupation and ruthless subjugation of Tibet, missile "tests" (i.e., the threat of nuclear annihilation) used to intimidate Taiwan, and the sale of nuclear technology and missiles to Pakistan. China's record concerning the rights of its own citizens is notorious—from forced abortions, to the massacre and imprisonment of thousands of protesters in Tiananmen Square in 1989, to the continuing imprisonment and torture of political dissidents. Economically, the Chinese government continues to engage in the wholesale pirating of intellectual property and the widespread use of slave labor, and its recent, partial liberalization is undercut by massive nepotism and corruption. Most ominously, Beijing seems intent on using China's recent economic expansion to finance a massive military buildup, targeted against the country it perceives as its chief rival and against which its intercontinental missiles are aimed: the United States.

The American Policy of Appeasement

How has President Clinton chosen to deal with this government of aggressive thugs? The one unchanging rule of the administration's policy is never to "endanger our relationship" with China—which means: to appease China's dictators at every turn. Instead of "isolating" China, Clinton holds, we must develop a "partnership" with it—a partnership maintained by our conferring on China the benefits of trade, technology, and cooperation. In return, the US gains only the illusion that these benefits will give us "leverage" with the Chinese leadership. But the minute it comes time to use our leverage, by withdrawing our benefits, the administration backs off—because this would "endanger our relationship" with China and deprive us of our "leverage." Who has leverage over whom in this arrangement?

The administration acts as if the best way of dealing with a criminal nation is not to threaten it with punishment, but to heap benefits on its head; not to brand it as a dangerous enemy, but to name it a "Most Favored Nation"; not to isolate it, but, in the summary of one press report, "to weave China into an international web of obligations." This callow policy is, unfortunately, not Clinton's invention and has nothing to do with the source of his campaign funds. It is standard US policy, going back to Nixon's "rapprochement" with China, the first act of which was to betray one of our best allies in the region by agreeing to sever diplomatic ties with Taiwan.

Our policy toward China comes from the same mentality that used to claim that "tensions" between the US and the Soviet Union were just the result of a "misunderstanding," and that the best way to protect ourselves against the Soviet threat was to prop up their dictators by supplying them with grain subsidies. It is the old policy of "détente," resurrected to deal with a new foe. As for altruism, it is only necessary to observe that our policy is in strict accord with the biblical injunction to "love thine enemy."

Copyright © 1999 Herblock at *The Washington Post*. Reprinted with permission.

At the root of this approach are the two cornerstones of current US foreign policy: pragmatism and altruism. Qua pragmatists, our foreign policy experts eschew any reference to ideas and principles to determine the source and nature of a nation's power. Instead, they are awed by the most brutishly concrete-bound considerations. China is a great and powerful nation that we must appease, they argue, because it is home to a vast mass of the world's population, i.e., to an enormous mountain of human flesh.

The most eloquent symbol of this policy in action is President Clinton's scheduled reception by Chinese leaders at a ceremony in Tiananmen Square. No more vicious example of surrender to evil could be offered than the spectacle of the leader of the free world shaking hands with China's dictators at the very site where they slaughtered their own citizens. How can Clinton possibly justify such a ceremony? According to a *New York Times* report, Clinton explained that "he could not dictate to China's leaders how they should receive a visiting head of state." The administration's self-abnegation is complete: It dares not make a single firm demand on China's leaders—not even to the extent of changing the location of a ceremony.

The United States Must Oppose Dictatorship

The tragedy is that the good is the more powerful—making the surrender to evil all the more inexcusable. China *does* need the United States. It needs our trade, our technology, and the moral sanction of being treated like a civilized nation. These things do give us enormous "leverage" over the Chinese. It is precisely for this reason that our appeasement of China is so cowardly and destructive. We are *volunteering* to aid and abet a hostile dictatorship, betraying our own interests and those of the freer nations that we should consider our allies.

If the US wants to take its own interests seriously, it should begin by using its leverage. It should inform the Chinese dictators that the condition for trade, cooperation, and friendly relations with the US is to free its own people and end its aggressive foreign policy. If they refuse to reform, we should recognize the leaders in Beijing as the brutal dictators and dangerous enemies they are—and treat them accordingly. The US should use its unmatched military and economic power—and its even more potent moral authority—to oppose, isolate, and undermine the current government of China. As the collapse of the Soviet Union demonstrated, this is the swiftest way of bringing about the defeat of China's dictatorship—and the only way to protect US interests.

6

| "U.S. policy toward China is the same policy
it has toward the rest of the world—namely,
it wants a Washington-centered world,
hegemony, to be the 'lone superpower.'"

The United States Should Not Try to Control China

Chalmers Johnson

Chalmers Johnson is president of the Japan Policy Research Institute and the author of *Blowback: The Costs of the American Empire*. In the following viewpoint, he argues that China has made considerable economic and political progress since it first became communist in 1949. In his view, many U.S. criticisms of China—on issues such as human rights or nuclear proliferation—are unjustified or exaggerated. Johnson maintains that much of the tension in U.S.-China relations is due not to China's actions, but rather to Americans' unease with China's emergence as a great power. Johnson warns that, to avoid conflict with China, U.S. leaders will have to accept that China is unwilling to let the United States be the dominant power in the Pacific region.

As you read, consider the following questions:

1. What are some of the criticisms that American politicians heap upon China, according to Johnson?
2. In the author's opinion, how would the People's Republic of China interpret an American pledge to defend Taiwan?
3. In Johnson's view, how is the debate over how to deal with China usually framed in the United States?

Excerpted from "In Search of a New Cold War," by Chalmers Johnson, *The Bulletin of Atomic Scientists*, September/October 1999. Copyright © 2000 by the Educational Foundation for Nuclear Science, 6042 South Kimbark, Chicago, IL 60637, USA. Reprinted with permission from *The Bulletin of Atomic Scientists*. A one year subscription is $28.

The news from China itself, 50 years after its revolution, is basically good. China is continuing to evolve in the same general direction as Taiwan, whose government was born under similar revolutionary and Leninist circumstances. The Chinese revolution of the twentieth century ranks with the French and Russian revolutions in terms of its aspirations and the ferocity of its ideology. It outclasses them in terms of the numbers of its victims—at least 30 million died as a result of a harebrained development scheme called the "Great Leap Forward."

However, compared with its decades of ideological and revolutionary activism under Mao Zedong, the leader who achieved victory for the communists, China today should not be difficult to live with. It has a centrally planned economy which is in the process of dismantling the institutions of state ownership and control it borrowed from its former ally, the Soviet Union. But it is trying to dismantle them in ways designed to avoid the pain and resentment that free market economics caused and continues to cause in Russia.

Regardless of the recommendations of foreign academics and banking theorists, China's leaders are devoted first and foremost to providing jobs for a huge population during a period of transition. At the same time, since the 14th Congress of the Chinese Communist Party in 1992, China has accepted the primary lesson of the East Asian "capitalist developmental states"—that the market under enlightened state guidance is a more powerful engine of development than either socialist displacement of the market or American-style laissez-faire.

China has started to emulate Asia's Japanese-type economies and is today the fastest growing economy on earth (it grew at a rate of 7.8 percent during 1998). Its people are also greatly enjoying this hitherto virtually unthinkable status. . . .

Yet Americans Complain

American criticism of China runs the gamut: Americans complain that China is not as environmentally sensitive as richer nations. They condemn the Chinese for selling arms to what Americans dub "rogue states"—even though Chinese sales do not come remotely close to America's own overseas arms sales, including to nations surrounding China. Some Americans like to say that China does not yet enjoy the "rule of law," even though many big American corporations are manufacturing there precisely because China does not have laws that protect workers from exploitation.

Grand strategists fault China because it retains a minuscule nuclear deterrent, even though the United States will not renounce its first-use policy and reserves to itself the right to reintroduce nuclear weapons into U.S. bases in Okinawa in times of military emergency in Korea or the Taiwan Strait.

Reflecting domestic social and moral controversies, some Americans with little interest in international politics condemn China's stringent birth control policies, even though with 1.2 billion people, China needs to do something. Others fault China for not welcoming various sects of the Christian religion into its midst, forgetting that a century ago Christianity was the handmaiden of Western imperialism, a fact the Chinese have certainly not forgotten.

In external affairs, the Chinese are at most pursuing irredentist claims—claims that are unquestionable in the case of Taiwan, more dubious but difficult to challenge in the case of Tibet, and in the South China Sea, moderated by its need to live with the only truly Asian international organization independent of Japanese and American influence, the Regional Forum of the Association of Southeast Asian Nations [ASEAN]. . . .

The Taiwan Controversy

Today, new Cold Warriors are greatly exacerbating tensions between mainland China and Taiwan through their incessant sabre-rattling. Some are doing so for partisan political advantage at home; others hope to profit by selling extremely expensive if unreliable arms in the area. Some are acting as paid lobbyists for Taiwan, which seeks to ensure that the United States would be drawn into any conflict, even if Taiwan's own policies provoked it. The United States would have no basis in international law for intervening on Taiwan's side in what is still an aspect of the not-yet-fully-resolved Chinese civil war, yet American provocateurs are leaking false intelligence reports, prodding Japan into closer military cooperation with the United States, and promoting the eventual deployment of theater missile defenses in the region.

China lacks the capability to invade and conquer Taiwan, but in its highly nationalistic domestic political climate, no government in Beijing could acquiesce in Taiwanese independence and survive. Mainland China may threaten to attack Taiwan with missiles to deter it from declaring independence, but it does not want to actually use its missiles because it understands that Taiwan would retaliate with massive force against mainland cities. The way to avoid conflict in the area is to perpetuate the status quo: continued self-government for Taiwan, but no formal declaration of independence. . . .

The Chinese Challenge to U.S. Hegemony

The United States is very eager to retain its position as the only superpower so as to maintain its dominant influence over the shaping of global development in the next century. . . . China, with its 1.3 billion people, has been developing in the last decade at an unprecedented speed. This simple fact is considered a potential challenge to the smooth functioning of U.S. strategic intentions.

In a way, this concern is understandable because ever since China's first encounter with the West, the world has been used to a weak, backward and, in the post-1949 years, isolated China. Now, for the first time, China is a rising power whose weight is to be reckoned with in the international arena. Yet, given the tremendous disparity in real strength and stages of development between China and the United States, most Chinese have difficulty understanding America's anxiety about and vigilance against China's further development. . . .

The United States is so accustomed to being far ahead of everybody else that the least sign that another country is narrowing the distance between them instinctively causes uneasiness.

Zi Zhongyun, *World Policy Journal*, Fall 1999.

From Beijing's point of view, Taiwan is the ultimate test of whether the United States is prepared to adjust to China's reemergence as a great power. An American pledge to defend Taiwan is actually an American pledge to go to war to keep China in a subordinate position. Arms sales to Taiwan—such as the sale of an advanced early-warning radar system that

Clinton agreed to in May 1999—do not actually enhance Taiwan's security. Any real threat of war would cause an instantaneous flight of people and capital from Taiwan into other areas of the Chinese diaspora, as occurred in 1996 when China and the United States faced off in the Taiwan Strait. American pledges to defend Taiwan would actually be destabilizing if China were to take them seriously. The only policy that makes sense is a hands-off approach that allows for quiet diplomacy—in other words, a continuation of U.S. policy since the Nixon-Kissinger breakthrough of 1972.

U.S. Hegemony

The debate in the United States today is whether to "engage" or to "contain" China. What is not being discussed is how to "adjust" to the reemergence of China as a great power.

Adjustment does not mean appeasement. And it is always possible that China will miscalculate and undertake some major initiative so damaging to the rights of others that U.S. retaliation would be appropriate. But the United States daily predicts such an outcome rather than undertaking diplomacy and statecraft to head it off.

I believe that the contradictions and inconsistencies of American policy toward China are not caused by conditions in China. U.S. policy toward China is the same policy it has toward the rest of the world—namely, it wants a Washington-centered world, hegemony, to be the "lone superpower," the "policeman of the world," the "reluctant sheriff" (the title of a Council on Foreign Relations book), "soft power," or any of the other euphemisms for a world order that is American-inspired, dominated, and led. The problem is that while American hegemonism vis-à-vis Germany, Japan, Latin America, Russia, and the United Nations results only in what [historian] Paul Kennedy has called imperial overstretch and long-term American decline, attempts at establishing American hegemony over China are doomed to failure from the outset.

Imperial overstretch can go on for a long time, only slowly undermining American pretensions, if all sides are careful to avoid confrontation. But an imperial attitude toward China will precipitate a crisis. China, the world's most populous nation, has only recently achieved an economy that promises to provide it with commensurate wealth and power. But China is also an old civilization, and its humbling by foreign imperialists over the past two centuries has instilled a powerful, nationalistic determination not to be humbled again. . . .

China does not owe obeisance to the United States. From 1950 to 1953, China and the United States fought to a stalemate in Korea. Post-war Japan may have been willing to exchange basing rights and public anti-communism for American transfers of technology and market access, but China does not have the same interests—although it does want the same access to the American market.

It has become increasingly apparent as the 1990s have progressed that there is something naïve about the popular American understanding of the Cold War as being aimed at Soviet communism and having come to an end with the dissolution of the Soviet Union. In the post-World War II world, the United States sought to do more than simply balance and check the power of the Soviet Union. It also sought to institutionalize American notions of democracy and free enterprise around the world.

This project did not end with the end of the Cold War. American leaders now openly say they would like to keep American troops in Korea even after North and South Korea are united, and that the NATO alliance is even more important without a Soviet adversary. During the mid-1990s, the main focus of American foreign policy in East Asia was enlarging and strengthening the military aspects of the U.S. alliance with Japan, even though military threats to Japan had become virtually nonexistent. These policies have been pursued in the face of both domestic Japanese and ASEAN skepticism and even hostility.

China Will Not Kowtow

In the United States, new villains are being created. The intent is not primarily to curb bad guys; it is to maintain American supremacy in political and economic terms around the globe. The Europeans and Japanese have often found it served their national interests to let the United States take the lead (Vietnam, the Gulf War, Taiwan Strait, Bosnia, Iraq), but the Chinese do not see the world that way. And the United States alone is no longer rich enough, or its people militaristic enough, to force China to kowtow. It is this conundrum that produces the serious disarray that surrounds all American discussions of China, revealing the contradictions embedded in the longstanding policies of hegemony and imperial overstretch.

The contradictions of American hegemonism have always been most evident in East Asia. Its Asian allies were not free-market democracies but developing states willing to trade verbal support of anti-communism for access to the U.S. market. Its Asian enemies—North Korea, China, Vietnam—were also not classic communist regimes, but anti-imperialist nationalists who fought with the fervor and staying power of patriots. As a result, the United States has not been militarily victorious in East Asia since 1945. Equally important, as soon as they recovered from war damage, its postwar Asian allies began to enjoy persistent trade surpluses with the United States, and the American economics establishment had to pretend that its trade deficits were the natural result of market forces rather than a consequence of the mercantilism and protectionism of its clients.

This pretense has started to come to an end because the Chinese economy is only incipiently some sort of capitalist economy and because China has no reason even to give lip service to the principles of American hegemony. It wants U.S. trade and investment, but it also wants a non-hierarchic relationship with the United States. China may be pursuing a Japanese-type strategy of economic development, but it does not want to repeat Japan's pattern of subservience to the United States. The emergence of China from its Leninist straitjacket and its adoption of market-based development policies is exposing many of the latent contradictions in American policy in the Pacific. The United States may need not only a new China policy, but a new policy toward all of East Asia and elsewhere. . . .

From a Chinese perspective, the United States seems to be overreacting to the possibility, even the likelihood, that China is emerging as the regionally dominant power. Not that China will physically dominate the region, but the U.S. role as sole arbiter of international events in the Pacific is coming to an end. The United States must learn to live in a multi-polar world, particularly in Asia.

Like Soviet specialists such as George Kennan, who warned that many Cold War policies merely fed traditional Russian paranoia about being encircled, I worry that current American suspicions about Chinese spying only confirm that nation's experience with Western imperialism and racism. As Christopher Layne, an international relations scholar and MacArthur Fellow, has observed, the pre-1914 relationship between Britain and Germany reminds us of what can happen when a dominant state refuses to accord a rising power the prestige and status to which it is entitled. Unfortunately, the U.S. bombing of the Chinese embassy in Belgrade, combined with its flaccid apology and refusal to produce those responsible, may have created the suspicion in China that the march toward a new Cold War is gaining momentum.

Periodical Bibliography

The following articles have been selected to supplement the diverse views presented in this chapter. Addresses are provided for periodicals not indexed in the *Readers' Guide to Periodical Literature*, the *Alternative Press Index*, the *Social Sciences Index*, or the *Index to Legal Periodicals and Books*.

Jodie T. Allen   "China's in the House," *U.S. News & World Report*, June 5, 2000.

Michael Barone   "China's Strait Flush," *U.S. News & World Report*, September 6, 1999.

Jagdish Bhagwati and Christopher Lingle   "Should China Be Allowed to Join the World Trade Organization?" *Insight on the News*, December 1, 1997. Available from 3600 New York Ave. NE, Washington, DC 20002.

Zbigniew Brzezinski   "Living with China," *National Interest*, Spring 2000. Available from P.O. Box 622, Shrub Oak, NY 10588-0622.

Steven Butler   "The Great Trade Wall," *U.S. News & World Report*, November 2, 1999.

Brian Duffy   "The China Conundrum," *U.S. News & World Report*, June 7, 1999.

Bates Gill   "Limited Engagement," *Foreign Affairs*, July/August 1999.

Issues and Controversies On File   "U.S.-China Relations," July 9, 1999.

John B. Judis   "Open Door: China Will Enter the WTO," *New Republic*, December 20, 1999.

Robert A. Manning and James J. Przystup   "Straits Jacket: 'One China' Policy," *New Republic*, September 27, 1999.

Arthur Waldron   "Bowing to Beijing," *Commentary*, September 1998.

Caspar W. Weinberger   "Taiwan Is the Victim—Not the Villain," *Forbes*, September 6, 1999.

World & I   "Does Taiwan Matter?" April 2000. Available from 3400 New York Ave. NE, Washington, DC 20002.

For Further Discussion

Chapter 1

1. The viewpoints by Lester R. Brown, Chenggang (Charles) Wang, and Wayne M. Morrison discuss the food scarcity, environmental, and economic problems facing China. According to the authors, in what ways are these three problems related?

2. In Robert D. Kaplan's view, how might each of the problems discussed in this chapter contribute to political instability in China?

Chapter 2

1. The U.S. Department of State argues that the Chinese government routinely violates rights that U.S. citizens take for granted. Abuses listed in the report include the arbitrary arrest and torture of citizens, censorship of the press, and persecution of religious groups. However, Ming Wan argues that the United States has ignored China's "silent majority," who, in her opinion, are willing to accept restrictions on their freedom if it will help their nation maintain political stability and achieve economic prosperity. In your opinion, is Wan's argument that the majority of Chinese people support their government persuasive? Do you feel that U.S. condemnation of China's human rights record is appropriate? Why or why not?

2. After reading the viewpoints by Harry Wu and by the Chinese government, do you believe that China's one-child policy is justified? Do you think that individuals have the right to have as many children as they want? Explain your answers.

3. Do you agree with William Saunders that trade sanctions should be imposed on China, or do you think David Dreier is correct in his argument that trade sanctions would most likely worsen China's human rights record? Defend your answer with evidence from the text.

Chapter 3

1. Based on the viewpoints in this chapter, do you agree with Frank J. Gaffney Jr. that the United States should work to "oppose the [Chinese] communist regime and work on bringing about its downfall," or do you feel that Henry Kissinger is correct in his assertion that a new cold war between the United States and China would be disastrous? Explain your answer.

2. Bates Gill and Michael O'Hanlon maintain that China's military poses little real threat to the United States. Do any of the argu-

ments made by Frank J. Gaffney Jr. or Mark Helprin persuade you that Gill and O'Hanlon could be wrong? If so, which ones?

Chapter 4

1. After reading the pair of viewpoints on Taiwan, do you agree with William Kristol and Robert Kagan that the United States has a responsibility to intervene should China attempt to take over Taiwan? Why or why not?

2. After reading the viewpoints in this chapter, do you agree with Robert W. Tracinski that the United States should "oppose, isolate, and undermine the current government of China," or do you agree with Jerry J. Jasinowski that engaging China economically and politically is the best way to influence the country? Explain your answer.

3. Robert W. Tracinski believes that U.S. foreign policy toward China is based on "appeasement." Chalmers Johnson argues that the main goal of U.S. foreign policy is to maintain U.S. "hegemony." Describe what the authors mean by these terms. Do you feel that U.S. policy toward China is best described by either of these authors? Might the truth be somewhere in the middle? Explain.

Chronology

221 B.C.   Much of what constitutes modern China is first united under the Qin dynasty.

206 B.C.–   After the death of the first Qin emperor and a
A.D. 220   brief civil war, the Han dynasty emerges. The imperial system and the bureaucratic administration developed under the Qin and Han dynasties provide a model for Chinese government for the next two millennia.

1298   Marco Polo, a Venetian explorer, writes a book about his travels in the Far East. His accounts of Oriental riches inspire other Western explorers.

1582   Matteo Ricci, an Italian Jesuit missionary, becomes the first foreigner permitted to live in Beijing.

1773   British traders begin paying for Chinese goods with opium rather than with Western goods or gold.

1839–42   The Opium War begins as China attempts to enforce its ban on Opium importing. The British respond by attacking several Chinese ports. The Chinese are easily defeated and the Treaty of Nanjing is signed in 1842. It stipulates that Chinese ports remain open to British trade and also cedes Hong Kong to the British.

1850   The Taiping Rebellion, the largest in Chinese history, begins as peasants revolt against the Qing dynasty. Not fully suppressed until 1864, the rebellion helps prepare the way for the end of the imperial system in the 20th century.

1856–60   A second Opium War pits China against Great Britain and France. It ends with the Chinese being forced to open more ports to trade with the West, legalize the importation of opium, and sanction Christian missionary activity.

1899–1902   The Boxer Rebellion occurs as antiforeign peasant groups known as Boxers attack Christian missionaries. An international force of British, French, American, German, Russian, and Japanese troops intervene, and China is ultimately forced to pay reparations to those countries and to permit foreign troops to be stationed in Beijing.

1911–12   The failure of the Boxer Rebellion triggers more support for anti-imperial revolutionaries. The imperial system collapses with the abdication of Emperor Henry Pu-yi, ending over two millennia of monarchy. Revolutionaries led by Sun Yat-Sen take over the government, and the Republic of China (ROC) is declared. The Kuomintang, also known as the nationalists, becomes the dominant political party of the new government.

1917   During World War I China joins the Allies and declares war on Germany.

1919   At the peace conference in Versailles, France, Chinese demands are ignored and the former Chinese territory of Kiaochow is awarded to Japan. The May Fourth Movement occurs as students, workers, and merchants protest. China refuses to sign the Treaty of Paris.

1921–23   The period of Sino-Soviet collaboration begins as the Communist International disseminates literature in China to start Communist groups. Disillusioned with the West, many Chinese respond and form the Communist Party of China (CCP). The CCP merges with the Kuomintang, creating a left and right wing in that party.

1926–28   Aided by the Soviet Union, the Kuomintang overthrows warlords in Beijing. Afterwards, disagreements break out between Kuomintang leader Chiang Kai-shek and the CCP. Chiang launches a purge of Communists, as Kuomintang troops destroy the CCP leadership in Shanghai.

1931   Japan occupies Manchuria, Mongolia, and north China. Chiang insists that the Kuomintang must purge the Communists before dealing with the Japanese threat.

1934   The CCP, led by Mao Zedong, begins the 5000-mile march to Shensi province to evade Chiang's extermination campaigns.

1945   World War II ends with the Japanese surrender to the Allies. China regains control of Manchuria and Taiwan.

1946–49	Communists (the CCP) and nationalists (the Kuomintang) battle for the right to govern China. On October 1, 1949, the People's Republic of China (PRC) is formally established with Mao Zedong as CCP chairman and leader. Remnants of the nationalist government flee to Taiwan, still calling themselves the Republic of China.
February 1950	China signs a 30-year treaty with the Soviet Union, granting the Soviets permission to station troops in China in exchange for loans, technical assistance, and return of part of the Manchurian territory.
1950–53	The Korean War begins with the United States and other United Nations (UN) members supporting South Korea, and China and the Soviet Union supporting North Korea. Clashes between Chinese and UN forces contribute to hostilities between China and the West.
1953–57	The Chinese government moves toward socialism with its first five-year plan, designed to model the Chinese economy after that of the Soviet Union.
1958	China begins the "Great Leap Forward," an attempt to quickly overcome the backwardness of China's economy. China moves away from the Soviet economic model as collective farms are combined into communes. However, the economic transformation is largely a failure and many Chinese starve to death as a result.
1959	The Soviet Union terminates its agreement to help China develop nuclear weapons. The Sino-Soviet split continues through the 1960s, as tensions between the two nations grow. In addition, widespread violence and rebellion in Tibet culminates in China forcing the Tibetan Buddhist ruler, the Dalai Lama, into exile.
1966–69	The Cultural Revolution, a radical movement aimed at transforming Chinese society, begins. In an effort to inspire the nation's youth and restore the fervor of the original 1949 Communist revolution, Mao orders all schools and universities closed as students form groups known as Red Guards. However, these groups defy orders and take over the government of Shanghai. Beijing

sends in the army to restore order, and China seems on the brink of anarchy for much of the Cultural Revolution.

1969   After clashes between the two nations on the Sino-Soviet border, China declares the Soviet Union its principal enemy, and the Soviets compare Mao to Adolf Hitler.

1971   The People's Republic of China gains membership in the United Nations and Taiwan loses its membership.

1972   President Nixon meets with Mao in Beijing and seeks to normalize relations between the United States and China. Twenty other countries establish diplomatic relations with the PRC; the United States is the only country to recognize the Republic of Taiwan as China.

1973   China begins to promote family planning.

1975   Chiang Kai-shek, the president of Taiwan, dies.

1976   Mao Zedong dies, and a power struggle within the Chinese government ensues. Moderate leader Deng Xiaoping emerges as a dominant leader, even though he holds no major government position.

1978   Deng Xiaoping initiates economic reforms, which include the dismantling of agricultural communes. These reforms continue throughout the 1980s, as the Chinese government reduces its control of the economy and permits more free enterprise.

1979   The United States and the PRC establish diplomatic ties. In the so-called Shanghai Communique, the United States ends its recognition of Taiwan and instead recognizes the People's Republic of China as the sole legal government of China.

1982   China's population reaches one billion.

1989   The Chinese government stages a bloody crackdown on prodemocracy protestors in Tiananmen Square in Beijing. In the ensuing political maneuvering within the Chinese government, Jiang Zemin emerges as the successor to Deng Xiaoping.

1994   President Clinton formally removes regulations that made the renewal of China's most favored nation status (later renamed normal trade relations status) contingent upon improvements in its record on human rights.

1996   Following the 1995 visit by Taiwanese president Lee Teng-hui to Washington, D.C., China conducts missile tests and other military exercises off the coast of Taiwan. Perceiving this as an attempt to intimidate Taiwan, President Clinton temporarily orders ships into the area in March.

1997   In accordance with the Sino-British Joint Declaration, signed by Great Britain and China in 1984, Hong Kong is returned to Chinese rule as a Special Administrative Region. Under the terms of the declaration, Hong Kong is to maintain a high degree of economic freedom until at least 2047.

1998   In June, President Bill Clinton makes the first U.S. presidential visit to China since Tiananmen.

1999   A series of incidents contribute to rising tensions between China and the United States. In March, reports surface that Chinese spies have stolen U.S. nuclear secrets. In May, the so-called Cox report lends authority to these claims. Also in May, during the air campaign against Yugoslavia, a U.S. bomber strikes the Chinese embassy in Belgrade. Chinese officials reject American claims that the bombing was an accident. In June, Taiwan president Lee Teng-hui declares that relations between Taiwan and the PRC should be conducted on a "state-to-state" basis, raising suspicions that Taiwan may declare itself independent from mainland China.

2000   In March, Chen Shui-bian is elected president of Taiwan. Chen is a member of Taiwan's Democratic Progressive Party, which has long advocated Taiwan's independence from mainland China. In April Chinese officials warn against a declaration of independence by Taiwan, but also offer that the island would be treated as an equal if its leaders accept the "one China" principle. On May 24, the U.S. House of Representatives passes legislation that would grant permanent normal trade relations (PNTR) status to China.

Organizations to Contact

The editors have compiled the following list of organizations concerned with the issues debated in this book. The descriptions are derived from materials provided by the organizations. All have publications or information available for interested readers. The list was compiled on the date of publication of the present volume; the information provided here may change. Be aware that many organizations take several weeks or longer to respond to inquiries, so allow as much time as possible.

American Enterprise Institute (AEI)
1150 17th St. NW, Washington, DC 20036
(202) 862-5800
website: www.aei.org

The institute is a public policy research organization dedicated to preserving and strengthening government, private enterprise, foreign policy, and national defense. Its Asian Studies Program focuses on the growing offensive capabilities of China's army, relations between Taiwan and mainland China, and economic and political reform in China. AEI's magazine, *American Enterprise*, often deals with developments in Asia, and the institute also publishes several books on China.

Amnesty International (AI)
322 8th Ave., New York, NY 10001
(212) 807-8400
website: www.amnesty.org

Amnesty International is an international organization that works to promote human rights. In 1999 it launched the "China: Ten Years After Tiananmen" campaign to raise awareness of the imprisonment of political dissidents in China. Details of the campaign are available on the group's website. AI also publishes an annual report detailing human rights violations around the globe.

The Asia Society
725 Park Ave., New York, NY 10021
(212) 288-6400
website: www.asiasociety.org

The Asia Society is an educational organization dedicated to fostering understanding of Asia and communication between Americans and the peoples of Asia and the Pacific. Its "AskAsia" website (www.askasia.org) is an online information source for students interested in Asia studies. Reports such as *The 2000 Taiwan Presi-*

dential Elections are available on its website, and the society publishes the book *China Briefing: The Contradictions of Change*.

Brookings Institution
1775 Massachusetts Ave. NW, Washington DC 20036
(202) 797-6000
website: www.brookings.org

Founded in 1927, the institution conducts research and analyzes global events and their impact on the United States and U.S. foreign policy. It publishes the quarterly *Brookings Review* as well as numerous books and research papers on foreign policy, including the conference paper "The Taiwan Dilemma: Time for a Change in the U.S. Approach?" and the report *Permanent Normal Trade Relations for China*.

CATO Institute
1000 Massachusetts Ave. NW, Washington, DC 20001-5403
(202) 842-0200 • fax: (202) 842-3490
website: www.cato.org

The Cato Institute is a conservative public policy research foundation that promotes the principles of limited government, individual liberty, and peace. Relations with China are a major research area within the institute's division of foreign policy studies. The institute publishes policy analysis reports and op-eds, including "China's Long March to a Market Economy: The Case for Permanent Normal Trade Relations" and "Chinese Nuclear Espionage: Is the Hysteria Warranted?"

Center for Security Policy (CSP)
1920 L St. NW, Suite 210, Washington, DC 20036
(202) 835-9077
website: www.security-policy.org

The center works to stimulate debate about all aspects of security policy, notably those policies bearing on the foreign, defense, economic, financial, and technology interests of the United States. It believes that China poses a threat to U.S. national security, and warns of this in many of its press releases and position papers.

Embassy of the People's Republic of China in the United States of America
2300 Connecticut Ave. NW, Washington, DC 20008
(202) 328-2500
website: www.china-embassy.org

The embassy provides news updates and white papers detailing the official Chinese government's positions on such issues as Taiwan, China's entry into the World Trade Organization, and human rights. Its publications include the white papers "The One-China Principle and the Taiwan Issue" and "The Progress of Human Rights in China," which can be found on its website.

Freedom House
1319 18th St. NW, Washington, DC 20036
(202) 296-5101
website: www.freedomhouse.org

Freedom House promotes human rights, democracy, free market economics, the rule of law, and independent media around the world. It publishes *Freedom in the World*, an annual comparative assessment of the state of political rights and civil liberties in 191 countries.

Heritage Foundation
214 Massachusetts Ave. NE, Washington DC 20002-4999
(202) 546-4400
website: www.heritage.org

The Heritage Foundation is a conservative think tank that formulates and promotes public policies based on the principles of free enterprise, limited government, individual freedom, traditional American values, and a strong national defense. It publishes many position papers on U.S.-China policy, such as "How Trade with China Benefits Americans" and "Time to Act on Taiwan's Security."

Hoover Institution
Stanford University, Stanford, CA 94305-6010
website: www-hoover.stanford.edu

The Hoover Institution is a public policy research center devoted to advanced study of politics, economics, and political economy—both domestic and foreign—as well as international affairs. It publishes the quarterly *Hoover Digest*, which often includes articles on China, as well as a newsletter.

Human Rights in China (HRIC)
350 5th Ave., Suite 3309, New York, NY 10118
website: www.hrichina.org

HRIC is an international nongovernmental organization founded by Chinese scientists and scholars. It monitors the implementation of international human rights standards in the People's Republic of China and carries out human rights advocacy and education among Chinese people inside and outside the country. HRIC's publications include the *China Rights Forum* as well as books, videotapes, and reports on the status of human rights in China.

Human Rights Watch
350 5th Ave., 34th Floor, New York, NY 10118-3299
(212) 290-4700
website: www.hrw.org
The goal of Human Rights Watch, an international advocacy organization, is to raise awareness about human rights and to investigate and expose human rights violations. It publishes the *Human Rights Watch World Report 2000* as well as special reports on China such as *China and Tibet: Profiles of Tibetan Exiles*.

Laogai Research Foundation
888 16th St. NW, Suite 5310, Washington, DC 20006
(202) 508-8215
website: www.laogai.org
The foundation is dedicated to collecting information about China's system of forced-labor camps. Its publications include the *Laogai Handbook* and the report *Killing by Quota, Killing for Profit: Executions and Transplants in China*.

Websites

CIA World Factbook: China
www.odci.gov/cia/publications/factbook/ch.html
This site offers extensive information on the geography, people, government, military, and economy of China.

Foreign Policy In Focus
www.foreignpolicy-infocus.org
This website offers briefings and reports on major developments in U.S. foreign policy.

U.S. Department of State China Homepage
www.state.gov/www/current/debate/china.html
This site provides news updates on U.S.-China relations.

Bibliography of Books

Claude E. Barfield and Mark A. Groombridge — *Tiger by the Tail: China and the World Trade Organization*. Washington, DC: American Enterprise Institute, 1999.

Richard Bernstein and Ross H. Munro — *The Coming Conflict with China*. New York: Knopf, 1997.

Paul J. Bracken — *Fire in the East: The Rise of Asian Military Power and the Second Nuclear Age*. New York: Harper-Collins, 1999.

Warren I. Cohen — *America's Response to China: A History of Sino-American Relations*. New York: Columbia University Press, 2000.

Elizabeth Economy and Michel Oksenberg, eds. — *China Joins the World: Progress and Prospects*. New York: Council on Foreign Relations, 1999.

Rosemary Foot — *Rights Beyond Borders: The Global Community and the Struggle over Human Rights in China*. New York: Oxford University Press, 2000.

John W. Garver — *Face Off: China, the United States, and Taiwan's Democratization*. Seattle: University of Washington Press, 1997.

Blake Kerr — *Sky Burial: An Eyewitness Account of China's Brutal Crackdown in Tibet*. Ithaca, NY: Snow Lion, 1997.

Samuel S. Kim, ed. — *China and the World: Chinese Foreign Policy Faces the New Millennium*. Boulder, CO: Westview, 1998.

Nicholas D. Kristof and Sheryl Wudunn — *China Wakes: The Struggle for the Soul of a Rising Power*. New York: Times Books, 1994.

Nicholas R. Lardy — *China in the World Economy*. Washington, DC: Institute for International Economics, 1994.

Nicholas R. Lardy — *China's Unfinished Economic Revolution*. Washington, DC: Brookings Institution, 1998.

Kenneth Lieberthal — *Governing China*. New York: W.W. Norton, 1995.

James Mann — *About Face: A History of America's Curious Relations with China, from Nixon to Clinton*. New York: Knopf, 1999.

James Mulvenon — *Chinese Military Commerce and U.S. National Security*. Santa Monica, CA: RAND Corporation, 1997.

Andrew J. Nathan

China's Transition. New York: Columbia University Press, 1999.

Andrew J. Nathan and Robert Ross

The Great Wall and the Empty Fortress. New York: W.W. Norton, 1997.

Jonathan D. Spence

The Chan's Great Continent: China in Western Minds. New York: W.W. Norton, 1998.

Jonathan D. Spence

The Search for Modern China. New York: W.W. Norton, 1999.

Edward Timperlake and William C. Triplett II

Red Dragon Rising: Communist China's Military Threat to America. Washington, DC: Regnery, 1999.

Edward Timperlake and William C. Triplett II

Year of the Rat: How Bill Clinton Compromised U.S. Security for Chinese Cash. Washington, DC: Regnery, 1998.

Ezra Vogel, ed.

Living with China: U.S.-China Relations in the Twenty-First Century. New York: W.W. Norton, 1997.

World Bank

China 2020: Development Challenges in the New Century. Washington, DC: World Bank, 1997

Harry Wu

Troublemaker: One Man's Crusade Against China's Cruelty. New York: Times Books, 1996.

Index

World Resources Institute, 38
World Trade Organization (WTO),
106
benefits of membership to China,
49–50, 51
membership of PRC in, will benefit
U.S., 64, 172–73
WTO. *See* World Trade Organization
Wu, Harry, 86

Yang Huan, 146

Yang Zhong, 82, 85
Ye Xiuying, 112

Zha Jianguo, 73
Zhang Youcai, 166
Zhu Qingping, 106
Zhu Rongji (PRC Premier), 41, 106,
126, 165
economic initiatives of, 47–48
Zhu Wenjun, 111
Zi Zhongyun, 184